Editor
Eric Migliaccio

Editorial Project Manager
Ina Massler Levin, M.A.

Editor-in-Chief
Sharon Coan, M.S. Ed.

Illustrator
Howard Chaney

Cover Artist
Jessica Orlando

Art Coordinator
Denice Adorno

Creative Director
Elayne Roberts

Imaging
Alfred Lau
James Edward Grace

Product Manager
Phil Garcia

Publishers
Rachelle Cracchiolo, M.S. Ed.
Mary Dupuy Smith, M.S. Ed.

Persuasive Writing
Grades 3–5

Written by

Rebecca Rozmiarek

Teacher Created Materials, Inc.
6421 Industry Way
Westminster, CA 92683
www.teachercreated.com
ISBN-1-57690-990-5

©2000 Teacher Created Materials, Inc.
Reprinted, 2004
Made in U.S.A.

Table of Contents

Table of Contents *(cont.)*

Introduction

Developing strong persuasive writing skills will help elementary school students meet with greater success in middle and high school. As children read stories, articles, and poems; watch TV and movies; play video games; and encounter an increasingly complex world, it is imperative that they are able to evaluate characters' actions, real-world issues, and current events. Even more importantly, children need to clearly articulate their evaluations to others by identifying their opinions and supporting their opinions with specific examples and details.

The persuasive writing activities in this book have been designed specifically for students in grades 3–5 and are divided into three categories of persuasive writing: letters, editorials, and reviews. This comprehensive book contains practical, step-by-step lessons designed to build skills in such areas as focusing the topic, selecting reliable sources of information, and appealing to the intended audience. Incorporated throughout the book are standards for assessment, writing process connections, student samples, and writing prompts that are ready for immediate classroom use. In addition, the rubrics throughout the book provide clearly defined criteria for evaluating the skills being taught. Included at the end of the book is a final assessment with cross-curricular connections.

Each lesson provides you with the student objective(s), standards for mastery, and the procedure for completing several activities. Each lesson also gives you many ideas for ways to extend the lesson by using portfolios, publishing, technology, home-school connections, and assessments. The section of the lesson entitled "Portfolio Piece" provides you with ways to get students to reflect on the strengths and weaknesses of their writing. The "Publishing" section of the lesson prompts you to organize celebrations of student work. The "Technology Connection" in each lesson offers ideas for doing research, revising, and enhancing text with graphics and fonts. The "Home-School Connection" provides ideas for linking what the students are learning in school with their lives outside of school. The "Assessment" section gives you ways to evaluate the students' work and determine if mastery has been achieved.

Finally, there is a strong learning thread woven throughout the book. Each section (writing letters, editorials, and reviews) contains 10 prompts which ask students to write to real audiences for the purpose of improving their schools and communities. By completing the lessons in this book, students will learn how to write well-developed letters, editorials, and reviews for the purpose of persuading their audiences to act in ways that benefit their schools and their neighborhoods.

Standards for Writing
Grades 3–5

Accompanying the major activities of this book will be references to the basic standards and benchmarks for writing that will be met by successful performance of the activities. Each specific standard and benchmark will be referred to by the appropriate letter and number from the following collection. For example, a basic standard and benchmark identified as **1A** would be as follows:

> **Standard 1:** Demonstrates competence in the general skills and strategies of the writing process
>
> **Benchmark A:** Prewriting: Uses prewriting strategies to plan written work (e.g., uses graphic organizers, story maps, and webs; groups related ideas; takes notes; brainstorms ideas)

A basic standard and benchmark identified as **4B** would be as follows:

> **Standard 4:** Gathers and uses information for research purposes
>
> **Benchmark B**: Uses encyclopedias to gather information for research topics

Clearly, some activities will address more than one standard. Moreover, since there is a rich supply of activities included in this book, some will overlap in the skills they address, and some, of course, will not address every single benchmark within a given standard. Therefore, when you see these standards referenced in the activities, refer to this section for complete descriptions.

Although virtually every state has published its own standards and every subject area maintains its own lists, there is surprising commonality among these various sources. For the purposes of this book, we have elected to use the collection of standards synthesized by John S. Kendall and Robert J. Marzano in their book *Content Knowledge: A Compendium of Standards and Benchmarks for K–12 Education* (Second Edition, 1997) as illustrative of what students at various grade levels should know and be able to do. The book is published jointly by McREL (Mid-continent Regional Educational Laboratory, Inc.) and ASCD (Association for Supervision and Curriculum Development). (Used by permission of McREL.)

Language Arts Standards

1. Demonstrates competence in the general skills and strategies of the writing process

2. Demonstrates competence in the stylistic and rhetorical aspects of writing

3. Uses grammatical and mechanical conventions in written compositions

4. Gathers and uses information for research purposes

Standards for Writing
Grades 3–5 *(cont.)*

Level II (Grades 3–5)

> **1. Demonstrates competence in the general skills and strategies of the writing process**

    A. Prewriting: Uses prewriting strategies to plan written work (e.g., uses graphic organizers, story maps, and webs; groups related ideas; takes notes; brainstorms ideas)

    B. Drafting and Revising: Uses strategies to draft and revise written work (e.g., elaborates on a central idea; writes with attention to voice, audience, word choice, tone and imagery; uses paragraphs to develop separate ideas)

    C. Editing and Publishing: Uses strategies to edit and publish written work (e.g., edits for grammar, punctuation, capitalization, and spelling at a developmentally appropriate level; considers page format [paragraphs, margins, indentations, titles]; selects presentation format; incorporates photos, illustrations, charts, and graphs)

    D. Evaluates own and others' writing (e.g., identifies the best features of a piece of writing, determines how own writing achieves its purposes, asks for feedback, responds to classmates' writing)

    E. Writes stories or essays that show awareness of intended audience

    F. Writes stories or essays that convey an intended purpose (e.g., to record ideas, to describe, to explain)

    G. Writes expository compositions (e.g., identifies and stays on the topic; develops the topic with simple facts, details, examples, and explanations; excludes extraneous and inappropriate information)

    H. Writes narrative accounts (e.g., engages the reader by establishing a context and otherwise creates an organizational structure that balances and unifies all narrative aspects of the story; uses sensory details and concrete language to develop plot and character; uses a range of strategies such as dialogue and tension or suspense)

    I. Writes autobiographical compositions (e.g., provides a context within which the incident occurs, uses simple narrative strategies, provides some insight into why this incident is memorable)

Standards for Writing
Grades 3–5 *(cont.)*

    J. Writes expressive compositions (e.g., expresses ideas, reflections, and observations; uses an individual, authentic voice; uses narrative strategies, relevant details, and ideas that enable the reader to imagine the world of the event or experience)

    K. Writes in response to literature (e.g., advances judgements; supports judgements with references to the text, other works, other authors, nonprint media, and personal knowledge)

    L. Writes personal letters (e.g., includes the date, address, greeting, and closing; addresses envelopes)

2. Demonstrates competence in the stylistic and rhetorical aspects of writing

    A. Uses descriptive language that clarifies and enhances ideas (e.g., describes familiar people, places, or objects)

    B. Uses paragraph form in writing (e.g., indents the first word of a paragraph, uses topic sentences, recognizes a paragraph as a group of sentences about one main idea, writes several related paragraphs)

    C. Uses a variety of sentence structures

3. Uses grammatical and mechanical conventions in written compositions

    A. Writes in cursive

    B. Uses exclamatory and imperative sentences in written compositions

    C. Uses pronouns in written compositions (e.g., substitutes pronouns for nouns)

    D. Uses nouns in written compositions (e.g., uses plural and singular naming words; forms regular and irregular plurals of nouns; uses common and proper nouns; uses nouns as subjects)

    E. Uses verbs in written compositions (e.g., uses a wide variety of action verbs, past and present verb tenses, simple tenses, forms of regular verbs, verbs that agree with the subject)

    F. Uses adjectives in written compositions (e.g., indefinite, numerical, predicate adjectives)

    G. Uses adverbs in written compositions (e.g., to make comparisons)

Standards for Writing
Grades 3–5 *(cont.)*

H. Uses coordinating conjunctions in written compositions (e.g., links ideas using connecting words)

I. Uses negatives in written compositions (e.g., avoids double negatives)

J. Uses conventions of spelling in written compositions (e.g., spells high frequency, commonly misspelled words from appropriate grade-level list; uses a dictionary and other resources to spell words; uses initial consonant substitution to spell related words; uses vowel combinations for correct spelling)

K. Uses conventions of capitalization in written compositions (e.g., titles of people; proper nouns [names of towns, cities, counties, and states; days of the week; months of the year; names of streets; names of countries; holidays]; first word of direct quotations; heading, salutation, and closing of a letter)

L. Uses conventions of punctuation in written compositions (e.g., uses periods after imperative sentences and in initials, abbreviations, and titles before names; uses commas in dates and addresses and after greetings and closings in a letter; uses apostrophes in contractions and possessive nouns; uses quotation marks around titles and with direct quotations; uses a colon between hours and minutes)

4. Gathers and uses information for research purposes

A. Uses a variety of strategies to identify topics to investigate (e.g., brainstorms, lists questions, uses idea webs)

B. Uses encyclopedias to gather information for research topics

C. Uses dictionaries to gather information for research topics

D. Uses key words, indexes, cross-references, and letters on volumes to find information for research topics

E. Uses multiple representations of information (e.g., maps, charts, photos) to find information for research topics

F. Uses graphic organizers (e.g., notes, charts, graphs) to gather and record information for research topics

G. Compiles information into written reports or summaries

Types of Persuasive Letters

Objective: The student will write a persuasive letter and identify the audience, purpose, and desired effect of the letter.

Procedure

1. Brainstorm topics for persuasive letters. Examples: family vacation, poor service in a restaurant, a defective product, etc.

2. Display on the overhead the corresponding reproducible entitled "Types of Persuasive Letters." This reproducible contains information about five different kinds of persuasive letters and the audiences and purposes for these letters. Have the students complete the bottom portion of the reproducible.

3. Instruct the students to choose one of the following prompts and respond:

   Prompt 1: Suppose your teacher is an excellent teacher who has been nominated to be "Teacher of the Year" in your school system. You have been asked to write a letter convincing the selection committee that your teacher is the best teacher. Remember to use examples to support your opinion.

   Prompt 2: Suppose you recently went out to eat at a nice restaurant, but you had to wait over an hour to receive your food—and when you did, it was cold. Write a letter of complaint to the owner of the restaurant expressing your concern about the quality of the food and service at the restaurant. Remember to use examples to support your opinion.

4. Have the students share their letters as a class and discuss with the students the audience, purpose, and desired effect of each of the letters.

5. Brainstorm with the students ways in which they could improve their neighborhood:

   - Saturday cleanup
   - providing activities for kids on holidays
   - gathering food and clothing for the needy

   Have the students each select an audience for their letter and write a letter convincing this audience to support the activity.

6. Have students use the "Types of Persuasive Letters" reproducible to create their own prompts. Then, have students switch prompts with their classmates and respond.

Types of Persuasive Letters *(cont.)*

Type of Letter	Audience	Purpose
To the Editor	—editor of a local newspaper, newsletter, magazine, TV news show —editor of a national newspaper, newsletter, magazine, or TV news show	• To share an opinion or ask a question about an article in a previous issue • To share an opinion about a local or national issue • To respond to a previous letter to the editor • To praise the editor about an article that was well-written
Request	—friends or family —manager at a company —principal or teacher —government official (congressperson, judge, police chief, mayor)	• To request information • To ask the audience to act on something • To ask the audience to investigate something • To ask the audience to improve a product, service, or decision
Complaint	—manager at a company —principal or teacher —government official (congressperson, judge, police chief, mayor)	• To tell the audience that you are not pleased with a product, service, or decision
Sales	—consumers	• To sell a product to a consumer
Recommendation	—manager at a company —school system (principal, teacher, or superintendent) —award selection committee	• To recommend a person for a job or acceptance to a school • To recommend a teacher, parent, or fellow classmate for an award

Identify the type of letter you write most often:_____

Brainstorm a list of topics for writing a business letter: _____

_____

Business Letter Format

Objective: The student will use business letter format and layout to write a persuasive letter to a given audience.

Procedure:

1. Use the "Types of Letters" reproducible on page 10 to review audiences and purposes that students could use for business letter writing. Brainstorm specific audiences and purposes with the students (for example: a letter to Principal Nancy Owensby recommending teacher Judy Sand as Teacher of the Year).

2. Display on the overhead the reproducible entitled "Parts of a Business Letter." Part I of this reproducible contains information about the six parts of a business letter: heading, inside address, greeting, body, closing, and signature. Pass out the "Examples of a Business Letter" on pages 13 and 14. Read the letters, identifying each part of the business letter as you read.

3. Have the students complete the "Student Practice" section at the bottom of page 12 in order to review the parts of a business letter.

4. Instruct the students to use proper business letter format to write a letter. Present the students with the following mini-prompts or use the prompts on pages 39–43 to encourage the students' thinking.

   —Write a letter of request to a company for free information about products.

   —Write a letter of complaint to a local store that provided you with poor service recently.

   —Write a letter to the editor about organizing a neighborhood cleanup. Remind students about choosing an audience and purpose.

5. Have the students use the "Business Letter Frame" on page 15 to write rough drafts.

6. Have the students use the "Business Letter Peer Response Form" on page 16 to give each other feedback on the content and format of their business letters.

Portfolio Piece: Have students include their letters in their portfolios. Have them each write a reflection in which they discuss whether or not the audience would be persuaded by their letter. "Remind them to use specific examples to support their claims.

Publishing: Have students mail their letters to the appropriate audiences.

Technology Connection: Have students use a word processing program, use a spelling and grammar checker, and select a font that is appropriate for a business letter.

Home-School Connection: Ask the students to think about an important school issue and discuss this issue with a family member. Have them each use the business letter format to write a letter to their principal about this issue.

Assessment: Use the rubric on page 17 to score the students' business letters.

Parts of a Business Letter

Directions: Read the following information about the parts of a business letter carefully and then complete the "Student Practice" at the bottom of the page.

Heading—This contains the full address of the writer, followed by the date.

Inside address—This begins two lines below the heading. Write Mr., Ms., Mrs., Dr., or Fr. before the audience's name and a comma and that person's job title after the audience's name. Then, write the full address of the audience.

Greeting—Begin this two lines below the inside address. Punctuate the greeting with a colon. "Dear" is the most common greeting.

Body—This begins two lines below the greeting. Remember to indent paragraphs. The body shows the writer's topic and purpose and provides at least two reasons to support the topic.

Closing—The closing begins two lines below the body and should line up with the left edge of the heading. "Sincerely" is a very common closing. Remember to capitalize the first letter of the closing and punctuate with a comma at the end of the word(s).

Signature—Type your name four lines below the closing. Then, write your signature (both first and last names) in pen between the typed name and the closing.

Student Practice

Match each of the following terms with the correct definition.

_____ 1. Heading

_____ 2. Inside address

_____ 3. Greeting

_____ 4. Body

_____ 5. Closing

_____ 6. Signature

a. "sincerely" is very common

b. main content of the letter

c. full address of the audience

d. greets the audience

e. handwritten and typed

f. full address of the writer

Example of a Business Letter

Recommendation

Directions: Read the sample business letter below. Use this example to help you write your own letter.

721 Winters Run Road
Millersville, MD 21211
January 23, 2000

Mrs. Nancy Owensby, Principal
Millersville School
3276 Anton Road
Millersville, MD 21211

Dear Mrs. Owensby:

I would like to recommend my teacher, Mrs. Judy Sand, for the Teacher of the Year award. Mrs. Sand has all of the personal qualities that make for a great teacher.

Mrs. Sand is very kind to all of her students. She always greets us each morning when we get to school. She smiles when she gives us our snack, and she waves goodbye each day when we leave school. In addition, Mrs. Sand always plans interesting lessons. Just the other day she taught us all about reptiles and amphibians. She made the lesson really fun when she had us dress up like reptiles and participate in a play. Finally, Mrs. Sand gives us lots of positive feedback on the work that we turn in to her. If we do a super job on a project, she puts a sticker on our work. We always know when we have done a good job.

Mrs. Owensby, please fill out the paperwork for nominating Mrs. Sand for Teacher of the Year. She truly deserves this award. I know you care about how the teachers in our school are educating the children. I can tell you from firsthand experience that Mrs. Sand is doing a great job. Thank you for considering my request.

Sincerely,

Jeremiah Jones

Jeremiah Jones

Example of a Business Letter

Complaint

Directions: Read the sample business letter below. Use this example to help you write your own letter.

703 Shamrock Court
Fallston, MD 21015
January 25, 2000

Pizza Dinners Unlimited
519 Ultimate Highway
Bel Air, MD 21014

Dear Manager of Pizza Dinners Unlimited:

Recently, I was in your pizzeria located on Forest Lane, and I was disappointed in the service that I received. It was last Sunday evening, September 19th, and I was in your restaurant with my family. We usually go out to dinner on Sunday evenings, and your pizzeria is one of our favorite places to eat. When we arrived, we waited about 30 minutes to be seated. When we were seated, we noticed that the seats and the table top were sticky. We told our server, but she did not clean the table or the seats.

As the evening continued, matters only got worse. We ordered drinks and waited about 15 minutes for them to arrive at our table. Unfortunately, the server spilled my brother's drink, a large diet soda, right in my dad's lap! The server did apologize and got a whole bunch of napkins for my dad to use to dry off. Then, we waited another hour for our pizza to arrive, and it was just a cheese pizza! (We had ordered a pepperoni pizza.) When the pizza arrived, it wasn't even cooked all the way through. The center of the crust was still frozen.

We were very surprised at the level of service that we received. Usually the food arrives on time and tastes good, the facilities are clean, and the servers are skillful at handling the food and drinks. We would like to continue to eat at your restaurant. Please visit your pizzeria located on Forest Lane and check into this matter. We are loyal customers, and you don't want to lose us. Thank you for your time and immediate attention to this matter.

Sincerely,

Jonathan Finkelstein

Jonathan Finkelstein

Business Letter Frame

Directions: Use this writing frame to write the rough draft of your business letter.

_____

_____

_____

_____

_____

_____

Dear _____

_____

_____

_____

_____

_____

_____

_____

_____

_____

Sincerely,

[Sign your name]

[Print or type your name]

Business Letter Peer Response Form

Writer's name: _____ Peer's name: _____

Directions:

❑ Read your draft aloud to your peer.

❑ Allow your peer to skim your letter for correct business letter format.

❑ Ask your peer the questions below about your letter.

❑ Take notes on what your peer says about how you can improve your draft.

❑ After you have completed this form, use a colored pencil to make necessary revisions based on your peer's comments.

1. Do I have all six parts of the business letter, and are all six parts correctly punctuated?

Heading	**YES**	**NO**
Inside Address	**YES**	**NO**
Greeting	**YES**	**NO**
Body	**YES**	**NO**
Closing	**YES**	**NO**
Signature	**YES**	**NO**

2. Is my letter correctly formatted on the page? How could I improve formatting? _____
_____
_____

3. Who is the audience for my letter? _____
_____
_____

4. What is the purpose of my letter? _____
_____

5. What are the two support reasons in my letter? _____
_____

6. Do you predict that my audience will be persuaded by this letter? Why or why not?
_____
_____

Rubric for a Business Letter

Writer: _____ Date: _____

Directions: Use the following rubric to check your business letter. Writers should evaluate their own letters in the "Self" column, peers should use the "Peer" column, and teachers should provide a final score in the "Teacher" column.

	Self	Peer	Teacher

Completeness

Heading
—full address of the writer and the date   (3)

Inside address
—audience's name, job title, and address   (4)

Greeting
—punctuated with a colon   (1)

Body
—purpose/opinion clearly identified   (1)
—clearly focused topic   (1)
—two reasons to support the purpose/opinion   (2)
—respectful tone toward the audience   (1)

Closing
—punctuated with a comma   (1)

Signature (typewritten and handwritten)   (2)

Formatting and Mechanics

—spacing between parts of the letter   (3)
—paragraphing   (2)
—spelling   (2)
—grammar   (2)

Total out of 25 points

Writer's Evaluation

The strengths of my letter are _____

_____

_____

Audience in Business Letter Writing

Objective: The student will use knowledge of the audience to write a persuasive business letter that meets the audience's needs and expectations.

Procedure:

1. Read aloud the reproducible entitled "Audience-Analysis Guide for Writing Business Letters."

2. Read aloud the business letter on page 13 and pause throughout the reading to discuss the clues the author gives about knowledge of the audience. Ask the students to find specific places in the text of the letter that show that the writer understands what Mrs. Owensby expects (e.g., the writer knows that Mrs. Owensby cares about educating students and how students are treated in the school building, the writer knows Mrs. Owensby deserves respect and therefore uses respectful words, etc.).

3. Instruct the students to identify a topic, audience, and purpose for their letters. Then, have them complete the "Audience-Analysis Guide for Writing Business Letters." Remind them to make inferences about the audience, if necessary.

4. Have students share analysis guides with peers to make sure responses are complete.

5. Have the students read business letters and discuss the "Audience-Analysis Guide for Writing Business Letters." Have the students identify which author did the best job appealing to the audience, using specific examples from the letters.

Portfolio Piece: Have the students identify examples from their persuasive letters where they used their knowledge of the audience and have them write a reflection on the importance of knowing the audience.

Publishing: Put the students in groups of four and have them read aloud their business letters. As each writer reads his/her letter, have the listeners record words or phrases that show knowledge of the audience.

Technology Connection: Write a business letter to the manager of an online company. Visit the Web site beforehand and then complete the audience analysis reproducible based on observations about the Web site.

Home-School Connection: Instruct the students to watch commercials on TV or find advertisements in a magazine. Ask the students, "What assumptions do advertisers make about their audience?"

Assessment: Evaluate the students on the completeness of the audience-analysis guides.

Audience-Analysis Guide for Writing Business Letters

Directions: Competent writers always have a "picture" in their minds of their intended audience. If you think about the audience before you write, you will be better able to write a letter that meets the audience's needs. Respond to the following questions in order to get to know the audience.

1. What is the age group of the intended audience? _____

2. What is the gender of the intended audience? _____

3. What is the highest level of education of the audience? _____
   _____

4. What is the audience's "job"? _____
   _____

5. Where does the audience live (city, rural, suburban, house, apartment, etc.)?_____
   _____

6. What does the audience already know about the topic(s) in the letter? _____
   _____

7. What will the audience want to know about the topic(s) in the letter?_____
   _____

8. What is the audience's greatest priority? _____
   _____
   _____

9. What information will be most persuasive to the audience? _____
   _____
   _____

10. What or who influences the audience (movie stars, athletes, bright colors, etc.)? _____
    _____
    _____

Addressing the Envelope for a Business Letter

Objective: The student will address an envelope for a business letter in order to mail the letter to the intended audience.

Procedure

1. Brainstorm with the students possible methods for getting a written message to an intended audience. Responses may include e-mail, U.S. mail, Federal Express, fax, hand delivery, etc.

2. Inform the students that they are going to learn how to send a letter by regular mail. Show the students the samples of addressed envelopes on the reproducible entitled "Examples of Addressed Envelopes for Business Letters."

3. On two large pieces of poster board, create a correct example of a business letter envelope and an incorrect example. Have the students identify which envelope is correct and which is incorrect. Then have them tell you how to create a correct version on the chalkboard or an overhead transparency.

4. Have students copy the address of the audience from the "inside address" of the business letter they have already written into the center of the rough draft envelope on the reproducible. Have the students write their names and their addresses in the upper left corner of the rough draft envelope.

5. Pass out blank envelopes and allow the students to address their envelopes.

6. Provide the students with telephone books and many rough draft envelopes. Have them look through the yellow pages, find addresses, and address the envelopes.

Portfolio Piece: Have students include the rough draft of their correctly addressed envelope in their portfolio and have them write a reflection in which they predict the outcome of correctly addressing their envelope.

Publishing: Make a bulletin board of correctly and incorrectly addressed envelopes. Allow the students to earn extra credit by correcting the incorrectly addressed envelopes.

Technology Connection: Demonstrate for the students how to create an address database. Demonstrate for the students how to use the computer to print addresses directly onto the envelope in preparation for mailing.

Home-School Connection: Have students collect examples of envelopes that they have received through the mail. Instruct the students to work with a family member to label correctly each of the parts of the envelope. Have the students bring them to school as examples for the bulletin board.

Assessment: Evaluate the students' ability to correctly complete the business letter envelope. To achieve mastery, students should correctly write their own address in the top left corner and correctly write the business address in the middle right of the envelope.

Examples of Addressed Envelopes for Business Letters

Example #1

Andre Perez
4926 Apore Street
La Mesa, CA 92103

Mr. Richard Allen, Manager
Southwest Grill
121 Indigo Avenue
La Mesa, CA 92103

Example #2

Elizabeth Martin
821 Old Fayettsville Road
Chapel Hill, NC 27516

Jocelyn Richards, Sales Manager
The Office Supply Store
2121 Sacramento Avenue
Richmond, CA 94804

Rough Draft Envelope for a Business Letter

_____
_____
_____

_____
_____
_____
_____

Standards and Benchmarks: 1A, 1B, 1C, 1D, 1E, 1G, 1L, 3K, 3L

Personal Letter Format

Objective: The student will use a personal letter format and layout to write a personal letter. The student will state the audience, purpose, and key points of a letter to a family member.

Procedure

1. Display on the overhead the reproducible entitled, "Parts of a Personal Letter." The first part of this reproducible contains information about the six parts of a personal letter: heading, inside address, greeting, body, closing, and signature. Pass out the "Example of a Personal Letter" on page 23 and read the letter, identifying each part of the personal letter as you read.

2. Have the students complete the "Student Practice" section at the bottom of page 24 in order to review the parts of a personal letter.

3. Instruct the students to use the proper personal letter format to write a letter to a family member. Present the students with the following mini-prompt or use the prompts on pages 39–43 to prod the students' thinking. Mini-prompt: Suppose you want to attend the play-off game for a local sports team. Write to a family member a persuasive letter that contains your request and at least two reasons to support your request.

4. Have the students use the "Personal Letter Frame" on page 25 to write a rough draft of their personal letters.

5. Have the students use the "Personal Letter Peer Response Form" on page 26 to give each other feedback on the content and format of their letters.

6. Pair the students and have them write personal letters to each other regarding favorite books they have read. Remind them to support their opinions with at least two reasons.

Portfolio Piece: Have students include their letters in their portfolios. Have them write a reflection in which they discuss whether or not the audience would be persuaded by their letter. Remind them to use specific examples to support their claims.

Publishing: Have students mail or give their letters to the appropriate audiences.

Technology Connection: Have students use a word-processing program to type their letters and instruct them to use the spelling and grammar checking functions to make sure that their letters are publishable.

Home-School Connection: Instruct students to go home and brainstorm a list of topics and audiences for persuasive personal letters. Possible audiences include parents, siblings, aunts, uncles, cousins, neighbors, and friends.

Assessment: Use the rubric on page 27 to score the students' personal letters.

Example of a Personal Letter

Directions: Read the sample personal letter below. Use this example to help you write your own personal letter.

2121 Cleveland Street
Gallitzen, PA 16641
September 3, 2000

Dear Mom,

I am writing this letter to convince you to take me shopping for school clothes. I would like to go this weekend and have a day with you to shop and go to lunch. There are many benefits to going shopping together this weekend.

First, as you know, my clothes from last year do not fit me very well. It will be important for me to be comfortable in school so that I can do my best on my school work. Additionally, I do not have any heavy sweaters and I know that I will need to stay warm during the upcoming frigid winter. I have been reading the store fliers, and I know that this weekend there are going to be big sales. We will be able to get my school clothes for a discounted price, which is always a plus. Finally, it will be a great way for us to spend some time together, just mother and daughter. Usually, our house is hectic, and I think it would be nice for us to have time to chat before the busy school year begins.

Thank you so much for taking my request into consideration. I appreciate all that you do for me.

Your daughter,

Julie

Parts of a Personal Letter

Directions: Read the following information about the parts of a personal letter carefully and then complete the "Student Practice" at the bottom of the page.

Heading—This contains the full address of the writer and the date.

Greeting—The greeting begins two lines below the inside address; punctuate it with a comma. "Dear [name]" is the most common greeting.

Body—This section begins two lines below the greeting. Remember to indent paragraphs. Paragraphs show the writer's topic and purpose and provide at least two reasons to support the topic.

Closing—This begins two lines below the body and should line up with the left edge of the heading. "Sincerely, [name]" is a very common closing. Remember to capitalize the first letter of the closing and punctuate with a comma at the end of the word(s).

Signature—The handwritten signature (usually first name only) goes a few lines below the closing.

Student Practice: Match each of the following terms with the correct definition:

_____ 1. Heading   a. handwritten a few lines below the closing

_____ 2. Greeting   b. paragraphs that support the topic

_____ 3. Body   c. begins two lines below the body

_____ 4. Closing   d. full address of the writer

_____ 5. Signature   e. "Dear [name]" most common

Personal Letter Frame

Directions: Use this writing frame to write the rough draft of your personal letter.

_____

_____

_____

Dear _____

_____

_____

_____

_____

_____

_____

_____

_____

_____

_____

_____

Sincerely,

_____

Personal Letter Peer Response Form

Writer's name: _____ Peer's name: _____

Directions:

❑ Read your draft aloud to a peer.

❑ Allow a peer to skim your letter for correct personal letter format.

❑ Ask your peer the following questions about your letter.

❑ Take notes on what your peer says about how you can improve your draft.

❑ After you have completed this form, use a colored pencil to make necessary revisions based on your peer's comments.

1. Do I have all five parts of the personal letter, and are all five parts correctly punctuated?

Heading	**YES**	**NO**
Greeting	**YES**	**NO**
Body	**YES**	**NO**
Closing	**YES**	**NO**
Signature	**YES**	**NO**

2. Is my letter correctly formatted on the page? How could I improve formatting? _____
   _____
   _____

3. Who is the audience for my letter? _____

4. What is the purpose of my letter?_____
   _____

5. What are the two support reasons in my letter?_____
   _____
   _____
   _____

6. Do you predict that my audience will be persuaded by this letter? Why or why not? __
   _____
   _____
   _____
   _____

Rubric for a Personal Letter

Writer: _____ Date: _____

Directions: Use the following rubric to check your business letter. Writers should evaluate their own letters in the "Self" column, peers should use the "Peer" column, and teachers should provide a final score in the "Teacher" column.

	Self	Peer	Teacher
Completeness			
Heading			
—full address of the writer and the date (3)			
Greeting			
—punctuated with a comma (1)			
Body			
—purpose/opinion clearly identified (1)			
—clearly focused topic (1)			
—two reasons to support the purpose/opinion (2)			
—respectful tone toward the audience (1)			
Closing			
—punctuated with a comma (1)			
Signature (1)			
Formatting and Mechanics			
—paragraphing (3)			
—spelling (3)			
—grammar (3)			
Total out of 20 points			

Writer's Evaluation

The strengths of my letter are _____

_____

_____

_____

Addressing the Envelope for a Personal Letter

Objective: The student will address an envelope for a personal letter with the purpose of mailing the letter to the intended audience.

Procedure

1. Brainstorm with the students possible methods for getting a message to the intended audience. Responses include: e-mail, U.S. mail, Federal Express, fax, hand delivery.

2. Inform the students that they are going to learn how to send a letter by regular mail. Show the students the samples of addressed envelopes on the reproducible entitled "Examples of Addressed Envelopes for Personal Letters."

3. On two large pieces of poster board, create a correct example of a personal letter envelope and an incorrect example. Have the students identify which envelope is correct and which is incorrect. Then have them tell you how to create a correct version on the chalkboard or an overhead transparency.

4. Have students copy the address of the audience from their address books or the address databases into the center of the rough draft envelope on the reproducible. Have the students write their names and their addresses in the upper left corner of the rough draft envelope.

5. Pass out blank envelopes and allow the students to address their envelopes.

6. Divide the students into partners and have them check each other's envelopes for correct layout and complete information.

Portfolio Piece: Have students include the rough draft of their correctly addressed envelope in their portfolio and have them write a reflection in which they predict the outcome of correctly addressing their envelopes.

Publishing: Make a bulletin board of correctly and incorrectly addressed envelopes. Allow the students to earn extra credit by correcting the incorrectly addressed envelopes.

Technology Connection: Demonstrate for the students how to create an address database. Demonstrate for the students how to use the computer to print addresses directly onto the envelope in preparation for mailing.

Home-School Connection: Have students collect examples of envelopes that they have received through the mail. Instruct the students to work with a family member to label correctly each of the parts of the envelope. Have the students bring them to school as examples for the bulletin board.

Assessment: Evaluate the students' ability to correctly complete the personal letter envelope. To achieve mastery, students should correctly write their own address in the top left corner and correctly write the audience's address in the middle right of the envelope.

Examples of Addressed Envelopes for Personal Letters

Example #1

Michelle Dubois
152 Hale Street
Beverly, MA 01915

Alexandra Royal
412 Trimble Fields Drive
Edgewood, MD 21040

Example #2

Thomas Paquin
1326 North Clayton Street
Wilmington, DE 19806

Edward Rosenthal
165 Shearer Road
Pittsburgh, PA 15239

Rough Draft Envelope for a Personal Letter

_____
_____
_____

_____
_____
_____
_____

Focusing a Topic

Objective: The student will ask questions about a broad topic with the purpose of narrowing that topic so that his/her persuasive writing is focused.

Procedure

1. Share with the students the following definition: *focus* is the main idea of the letter. It is important for authors to maintain focus (consistently support the main idea) so that the reader understands the author's purpose.

2. Read aloud the two examples of business letters on page 13 and 14 and ask students to listen for the main idea or focus of each letter.

3. On the board or overhead, identify the author's focus in each letter. Then identify subtopics from each letter that support and elaborate on the main idea. Every subtopic should support the author's main focus.

4. Have students brainstorm a number of broad topics (examples: shopping, weather, animals, family, travel, education, government, school, etc.)

5. Have students answer the questions on the reproducible entitled "Asking Questions to Focus a Topic." As students complete the worksheet, circulate and guide them as they focus their broad topics. Encourage students to think carefully about what interests them about the topic. When students are interested in the topic, it will motivate them to maintain focus.

6. Read newspaper or magazine articles and discuss the strengths of each of the articles in terms of the author's ability to maintain focus.

Portfolio Piece: Instruct students to use their focus worksheets to write business letters or other pieces of persuasive writing. Have the students write a reflection in which they identify their focus and the process they used to select details that support the focus.

Publishing: Post the students' business letters on the bulletin board. Make sure the students highlighted the focus or main idea of their letters. Have them highlight in a different color all of the details that directly support the focus of the letter.

Technology Connection: Have students use their focus worksheets to write e-mail messages about the topic to their friends. Have students ask their e-mail buddy to answer the question, "What is the focus of this e-mail message?"

Home-School Connection: Instruct the students to each use the focus questions during a phone conversation with a family member in order to focus the topic being discussed.

Assessment: Read the students' worksheets ("Asking Questions to Focus a Topic") and assess whether or not they each included enough detail for each question.

Asking Questions to Focus a Topic

Directions: Use the questions below to focus the topic of a business letter or other persuasive piece of writing.

Broad Topic _____:

1. What do I already know about this topic? List two or more things. _____

   _____

   _____

   _____

2. What do I want to learn about this topic? What questions do I have about this topic?
   List two questions. _____

   _____

   _____

   _____

   _____

3. Which question is the most interesting to me? Why? _____

   _____

   _____

   _____

4. What resources do I have available to me in order to learn more about this topic? _____

   _____

   _____

   _____

5. Who can I interview about this topic or issue? _____

   _____

   _____

   _____

6. Focused Topic (write as a question): _____

   _____

   _____

   _____

Supporting an Opinion

Objective: The student will support an opinion with detailed evidence citing appropriate sources of information.

Procedure

1. On the chalkboard or overhead, define the word *opinion* for the students. An opinion is what the author believes about the topic.

2. Present the students with the following statements: Endangered animals should be protected. (Topic: Animals) Reading many books and magazines will make you a better reader. (Topic: Reading) Instruct students to choose one of the above statements to support or oppose.

3. After students have chosen a statement, have them fill out the reproducible entitled "Supporting an Opinion." Guide the students when they are writing their opinion statements. Have them use the following sentence starter: I am writing this letter to convince you that. . . .

4. Guide students when they write the reasons for their opinion statements. Inform the students that reasons can include well-known facts, examples from personal experience, logical reasons, examples from text, and expert opinions (gained through research or interviews).

5. Divide the students into pairs and have them read each other's letters and look carefully for a clear opinion statement and adequate supporting reasons.

Portfolio Piece: Have students include their letters in their portfolios. Instruct them to write a reflection in which they identify the strengths and weaknesses of their letters.

Publishing: Divide students into pairs. Have each pair take opposing sides on an issue and debate that issue in front of the class. Students will need to research their key points, anticipate the key points of their opponents, and plan counter arguments.

Technology Connection: Have students each send an e-mail message to a friend. Instruct the students to each include in their e-mail message a question in which they ask their friends whether or not they included adequate support for their ideas. Share responses in class.

Home-School Connection: Instruct students to each write a letter to a family member requesting a favorite meal. Have the students each include their opinion of this meal and support their opinion with detailed examples and reasons. Discuss in class whether or not family members complied with the requests and why.

Assessment: Use the rubric for evaluating a business letter on page 17 to score the students' letters for using examples to support their opinions.

Supporting an Opinion *(cont.)*

Directions: Use this graphic organizer as a brainstorming tool for your letter. The stronger your details are, the more persuasive your letter will be.

Topic: _____

Audience: _____

Purpose:_____

_____

_____

Your opinion: I am writing this letter to convince you that _____

_____

_____

_____

Supporting details for the opinion (may include well-known facts, examples from personal experience, logical reasons, examples from text, and expert opinion gained through research or interviews):

Detail #1

Detail #2

Detail #3

Standards and Benchmarks: 1A, 1B, 1C, 1D, 1G, 1K, 1L, 3K, 3L

E-mail Correspondence

Objective: The student will write and send an e-mail message intended to persuade the audience about a specific topic.

Procedure

1. Read a story to the class and have each student develop a response to the questions "Did you enjoy the story? Why or why not?" Students will each need at least two specific details to support their opinion.

2. Partner the students with e-mail buddies who have read the same story. E-mail buddies could be from a class within the school or from a class at another school.

3. Have the students plan their e-mail messages. Instruct them to use the reproducible entitled "Planning an E-mail Message" to write a persuasive letter to their buddies about whether or not they liked the story they read. Remind the students that they each need a good topic sentence and supporting details.

4. Take students to the school computer lab and show them how to complete the address, subject, and message portion of an e-mail correspondence.

5. Record a brief summary of the buddy's response in the buddy portion of the reproducible. Buddies should agree or disagree, citing examples from the story.

6. Discuss with the students the correct e-mail etiquette. Examples include not using all capital letters; continuing to use greetings, closings, and capital letters at the beginnings of sentences and correct end marks at the ends of sentences; and limiting the use of "smiley faces" and other cyber icons intended to show emotion.

Portfolio Piece: Have students each print one of their e-mail messages and include the message in their portfolio. Have the students each write a reflection on whether or not they used adequate support when presenting their opinions. Instruct them to use "Planning an E-mail Message" for reference.

Publishing: Create a bulletin board and post students' e-mail messages and their buddies' responses.

Technology Connection: Show students how to set up an "e-mail address list" to keep track of their e-mail buddies, friends, and other family members online.

Home-School Connection: Encourage students to get Internet access and set up e-mail addresses at home. Inform parents about how to guide students when researching on the Web. Inform parents about blocking devices to protect students from inappropriate information.

Assessment: Evaluate the students' ability to plan and send their e-mail messages properly.

Planning an E-mail Message

E-mail Address of the Receiver: _____

Subject of the Message: _____

Message: _____

Dear _____,

I (enjoyed/did not enjoy) the story entitled _____ because . . .

Reason #1:

Reason #2:

Reason #3:

Buddy's Response: Was your buddy persuaded by your e-mail message? How do you know?

_____

_____

_____

_____

Using End Marks Correctly

Objective: The student will use end marks correctly in both personal and business letters.

Procedure

1. Inform the students that they will be learning how to use correct end marks for sentences. For many students this will be a review.

2. Pass out the reproducible entitled "Using End Marks." Read aloud to the students the definitions of the three different end marks and allow the students time to complete the "Writer's Practice" section of the reproducible.

3. Have the students reread the business letters or personal letters that they have written. Have them highlight all of their end marks and then go back, reread what they have written, and determine if they have used end marks correctly in their writing.

4. Instruct students to switch papers with a partner. Have students read each other's papers and determine the correctness of the end marks used. Students should make editing changes directly on their papers.

5. Have the students read articles and editorials and highlight the end marks. Instruct the students to determine whether or not the authors of these texts used end marks correctly.

Portfolio Piece: Have the students each include a reflection in their portfolio in which they identify the importance of using end marks correctly. Students should be able to explain that writers use end marks to signal to the reader when one thought ends and another one begins.

Publishing: Create a bulletin board with a chart that has three different categories: periods, exclamation points, and question marks. Give students colorful sentence strips and have them compose sentences to post in each of the categories of the chart.

Technology Connection: Remind students that when they are typing sentences, they need to put two spaces after the end mark of a sentence.

Home-School Connection: Have students read with a family member business letters that come in the mail. Junk mail would be appropriate for this activity. Have the students identify the end marks used in the letters and discuss whether or not the authors used end marks appropriately.

Assessment: Evaluate the students' ability to complete the 15 sentences in the "Writer's Practice" section of the reproducible "Using End Marks." Read the students' letters and determine whether they applied their knowledge of end marks to their own writing.

Using End Marks

Directions: Read the information about end marks below. Then punctuate the sentences correctly in the section entitled "Writer's Practice."

Period—The period is used at the end of a statement.

Exclamation Point—The exclamation point is used to express excitement or emphasis for an important point. Exclamation points should be used sparingly.

Question Mark—The question mark is used at the end of a question.

Writer's Practice: Put the correct end mark at the end of each of the following sentences.

1. Run _____ There is a bear behind you _____

2. When are you going to the store _____

3. The red car turned the street corner _____

4. The sky is very blue today _____

5. George Washington was the first president of the United States _____

6. Wow _____ I can't believe I won _____

7. Where is the soda that I just brought in from the car _____

8. The package from the store just arrived _____

9. Why is their note in our mailbox _____

10. Ouch _____ Stubbing my toe really hurt _____

11. How are you going to get to the baseball game _____

12. What is the name of your dog _____

13. How fast can you run _____

14. It is time for me to take a break and go for a drive _____

15. There is a blizzard outside, and a foot of snow has accumulated _____

Responding to Prompts for Letter Writing

Objective: The student will respond to a letter writing prompt by using the proper letter writing format and supporting an opinion with examples.

Procedure

1. Use the previous lessons in the letter writing section to teach the students how to format and organize their letters and support their opinions with examples. Show students the rubrics for letter writing on pages 17 and 27 in order to demonstrate to them how their letters will be evaluated.

2. Pass out one of the letter writing prompts and instruct the students to respond to the corresponding "Quick Write." Students should respond to this question as quickly as possible because it is intended to stimulate the students' thinking. (Tip: Give the students a time limit to respond to the "Quick Writes.")

3. Instruct the students to respond to the prompt. Guide and encourage the students as they are drafting their responses.

4. Have students use the peer response forms on pages 16 and 26 to respond to the drafts.

5. Instruct the students to revise and redraft, as necessary, in order to produce publishable drafts.

6. Divide the students into pairs and have them engage in a role-playing scenario in which one student is the author of the letter and the other student is the audience of the letter. Have the student who is portraying the "audience" ask the writer for clarification on different points in the letter.

Portfolio Piece: Have students respond to many of the prompts and each choose their favorite to include in their portfolios. Have them each write a reflection in which they give reasons for their choice with examples from the text of their letters.

Publishing: Have the students share their letters with the class and celebrate the things they did well (using examples, being respectful to the audience, etc.). Instruct the students to mail their letters directly to their intended audiences.

Technology Connection: Have students e-mail their letters as attached files to their intended audiences.

Home-School Connection: Instruct students to select one of the prompts with a family member and brainstorm possible responses.

Assessment: Depending on the audiences for the prompts, use the rubric for a business letter on page 17 or the rubric for a personal letter on page 27 to evaluate the students' responses to the prompts.

Prompts for Letter Writing

Prompt #1: Planning a Fund-Raiser

Quick Write: Brainstorm five things you could do to improve your school by using the money from a fund-raiser.

Suppose you and your classmates want to plan a fund-raiser to raise money for your school. Write a letter to your principal that describes your plan and supports your opinion with two or three reasons. You might want to include a description of the product or service that you would sell, your target audience for the product or service, and information about the fund-raising company you would like to use. Additionally, you will want to include your purpose for fund-raising (examples include sponsoring an educational field trip or purchasing books, materials, or technology for your school). Remember to develop your ideas completely and clearly. In addition, remember to think about what you know about the audience and to maintain a respectful tone throughout your letter.

Prompt #2: Requesting a Visit from a Favorite Author

Quick Write: List three reasons you would like your favorite author to speak at your school.

Suppose you and your classmates want to invite a favorite author to your school to speak to students about his/her writing. Write a letter to this author requesting a visit to your school and support your request with two or three reasons. In your letter, you might want to include the titles of the author's books that you have read and enjoyed, the things that you have learned from this author's books, and questions you have about being a better writer. Remember to develop your ideas completely and clearly. In addition, remember to think about what you know about the audience and to maintain a respectful tone throughout your letter.

Prompts for Letter Writing *(cont.)*

Prompt #3: Nominating a Teacher for an Award

Quick Write: Brainstorm five qualities that great teachers have.

Suppose you and your classmates want to nominate one of your favorite teachers for a teaching award. Write a letter to your principal that describes your plan and supports your opinion with two or three reasons. You might want to include a description of the teaching techniques of your favorite teacher, his/her attitude toward students, and special things that your favorite teacher does throughout the year to make learning fun. Remember to develop your ideas completely and clearly. In addition, remember to think about what you know about the audience and to maintain a respectful tone throughout your letter.

Prompt #4: Requesting Improved Technology for Your School

Quick Write: List three kinds of technology that would be beneficial to your school.

Suppose you and your classmates want to write a letter to a school official requesting an improvement in the technology in your school. In your letter to the school official, support your opinion with two or three reasons. You may want to include how technology will improve students' ability to conduct research, their ability to produce polished pieces of writing, and their ability to incorporate professional graphics and other design elements. In addition, you may want to include how technology will improve the teachers' ability to present information to students in interesting ways that capture their attention. Remember to develop your ideas completely and clearly. In addition, remember to think about what you know about the audience and to maintain a respectful tone throughout your letter.

Prompts for Letter Writing *(cont.)*

Prompt #5: Planning a Family Activity Night

Quick Write: Give three reasons for planning a Family Activity Night at your school.

Suppose you and your classmates want to plan a Family Activity Night at your school. Write a letter to your principal describing your plan and supporting your opinion with two or three reasons. You might want to include a list of the games that you want to play, the foods that you want to serve, and the music you intend to play. Remember to develop your ideas completely and clearly. In addition, remember to think about what you know about the audience and to maintain a respectful tone throughout your letter.

Prompt #6: Recommending a Favorite Restaurant

Quick Write: Pick one restaurant and give three reasons why it is your favorite.

Suppose you want to recommend a favorite restaurant to a friend. Write a letter to your friend and include two or three reasons why he or she should eat at this restaurant. Begin your letter by identifying the restaurant and include the kind of foods and appetizers that are served, the atmosphere of the restaurant, and the location. Make sure to include sensory details and adjectives in your description of the food in order to make it as appealing as it is at the restaurant. Remember to develop your ideas completely and clearly. In addition, remember to think about what you know about the audience and to maintain a respectful tone throughout your letter.

Prompts for Letter Writing (cont.)

Prompt #7: Expressing Dissatisfaction with a Service

Quick Write: List three kinds of service. (Examples include mail delivery, newspaper delivery, gas, electric, telephone, and service in a restaurant.)

Suppose you have been displeased with one of the services that you brainstormed. Write a letter to the manager expressing your dissatisfaction. Plan and support your opinion with two or three reasons. You might want to describe your problem with the service, why the service is important to you, and whether or not you plan to take your business elsewhere as a result of the poor service. Remember to develop your ideas completely and clearly. In addition, remember to think about what you know about the audience and to maintain a respectful tone throughout your letter.

Prompt #8: Asking for a Drama Club

Quick Write: List five benefits a drama club would provide for students.

Suppose you and your classmates want to perform plays after school for your friends, family, and local community members. You decide you want to start a drama club. Write a letter to your teacher in which you clearly state your request and list two or three reasons why you want to start the drama club. You may want to include a proposed name for the club, the entertainment and educational value of starting a club, the benefits to the school and the community, and any costs involved. Remember to develop your ideas completely and clearly. In addition, remember to think about what you know about the audience and to maintain a respectful tone throughout your letter.

Prompts for Letter Writing *(cont.)*

Prompt #9: Planning an End-of-the-Year School Trip

Quick Write: Brainstorm five educational places that you would like to go for an end-of-the-year school trip.

Suppose you and your classmates want to plan an end-of-the-year trip to the zoo, aquarium, museum, a wildlife preserve, or another educational attraction. Write a letter to your teacher describing how you and your classmates will benefit personally and academically from this trip. You will also want to include a plan for chaperones, lunches, and a budget for the trip with ideas for how to pay for it. Your letter should include two or three reasons to support your plan. Remember to develop your ideas completely and clearly. In addition, remember to think about what you know about the audience and to maintain a respectful tone throughout your letter.

Prompt #10: Planning a Community Service Project

Quick Write: List five possible community service projects you could do in your area and tell why they are important for the community.

Suppose you and your classmates have a good idea for a local community service project. (Examples include cleaning up the neighborhood, a community leaf rake, a trip to the soup kitchen, visiting the senior citizen's center, or reading to little kids at the local library or day-care center.) Write a letter to your teacher describing the project and include two or three reasons supporting your request. You may want to include how this project will benefit the local organization, the school community, and you personally by teaching you how to be a contributing member of the community. Remember to develop your ideas completely and clearly. In addition, remember to think about what you know about the audience and to maintain a respectful tone throughout your letter.

Criteria for Writing an Editorial

Objective: The student will identify the criteria of an editorial and use those criteria to read sample editorials and write an original editorial.

Procedure

1. Write the definition of an editorial on the overhead or chalkboard: An *editorial* is a persuasive essay written by the editor of a newspaper or magazine. The content of an editorial deals with topics that are important to the audience of the newspaper or magazine.

2. Inform the students that an editorial satisfies the following criteria:

   • a clever beginning (personal experience story, rhetorical question, scenario, "imagine that" phrase, etc.)

   • an opinion on an issue that is important to the audience

   • support for the opinion

   • a strong conclusion that wraps up key points

3. Have students read the "Example of an Editorial About a Community Issue" and identify the criteria in the sample editorial. Use the following questions to guide your discussion: Does the beginning grab your attention? What is the writer's opinion on the issue? What support does the writer provide to back up his/her opinion? Is there a strong conclusion?

4. Use the editorial prompts on pages 95–99 for student responses.

5. Use the "Peer Response Form for an Editorial" on page 47 for the students to give each other feedback on their editorials.

6. Use the "Self" and "Peer" sections of the "Rubric for an Editorial" on page 48 to allow the students an opportunity to evaluate their own editorials.

Portfolio Piece: Have students include their editorials in their portfolios. Have them reflect on how they developed their opinions and included strong supporting details.

Publishing: Provide students with the opportunity to publish their editorials in a class newsletter. Have a round-robin oral reading of editorials. Have students give praise for the strongest criteria for each editorial that is read.

Technology Connection: Examine editorials that are published in magazines or newspapers. Cut out excellent examples. Have students use a word-processing program to format their editorials to resemble excellent published examples.

Home-School Connection: Instruct students to read editorials in the local newspapers and discuss with a family member the editor's fulfillment of editorial criteria.

Assessment: Use the "Rubric for an Editorial" on page 48 to evaluate the students' editorials.

Example of an Editorial About a Community Issue

Directions: Read the following editorial carefully and think about the criteria of an editorial. Be prepared to discuss with your teacher the criteria of an editorial after you read.

When schools promote community service projects, students learn how to protect their environment, take care of younger kids, assist those who may face unfortunate circumstances, and stay connected with senior citizens. Community service projects help students learn how to take care of the world that will eventually be theirs to manage. Our school, The Bakerfield School, has participated in several community service projects during the past school year.

In the fall, the intramural sports teams sponsored a community leaf rake. It was great to see boys and girls raking the leaves of the houses that surround the school. When they were finished, the yards were clear of leaves, and neighbors were very grateful for their clean lawns.

In home economics classes, students participated in babysitting courses. While many students in our school are not old enough to babysit for neighbors, many Bakerfield students frequently take care of younger siblings. During the babysitting courses, students learned safety techniques, entertainment tips, and ways to make quick and easy meals without having to turn on the stove or oven. Parents were extremely grateful that students were learning productive ways to help with the care of younger siblings.

During the cold winter months, students visited local soup kitchens to help prepare meals. Additionally, students and their families donated blankets and winter coats to those in need. It is important that we help those who may be struggling to make it through the winter.

In the spring, students took a field trip to the local senior citizens center to read books and play board games with the residents. Students greatly benefited from the opportunity to hear stories from the residents' lives. The residents were extremely grateful for the company and made the students promise to visit again.

Our school has worked hard to participate in making our community a better place to live. We know that it is important that we preserve our future by taking care of what we have now. Please spread the word. Make your school a school committed to community service projects.

Example of an Editorial About a School Issue

Directions: Read the following editorial carefully and think about the criteria of an editorial. Be prepared to discuss with your teacher the criteria of an editorial after you read.

Have you ever wondered what the schools of the future will be like? What kind of high-tech equipment will teachers have in order to make learning more engaging for students? Unless we increase the technology budget at our school, we will never know. It is time for the school's budget committee to make a list of our technology needs and fund a budget for improving the technology in our school.

Here are some proposed uses for the money. We need to make sure that every teacher has a computer and a printer for planning lessons, creating a grade database, and allowing students to do word processing and use various educational software programs. We also need to provide a TV and VCR to every teacher so that teachers can show videos that are relevant to the curriculum. Additionally, there should be two full-size computer labs with Internet access in every school. In the library, there should be at least 20 computers with Internet access. Finally, we need to fund increased teacher training so that teachers know how to use the software programs and the Internet, which will make managing the classroom and implementing lessons easier and more engaging for students.

Certainly, this kind of technology will cost a lot of money, and there will be those who criticize this use of financial resources; but if we are not preparing students to use cutting edge technology, then how will our country move forward? If students are proficient with word-processing programs and research using the Internet by the time they leave elementary school, then students will be better able to meet with success the demands in middle school and beyond. But if they don't have access to the technology, then it is not possible for them to gain these necessary skills.

I ask that all teachers, students, parents, and government officials support an increase in the technology budget. Let's help our school start the 21st century equipped with the technology necessary to help all of our students be high achievers.

Peer Response Form for an Editorial

Writer's name: _____ **Peer's name:** _____

Directions

❏ Read your draft aloud to your peer.

❏ Allow your peer to skim your editorial for the correct criteria.

❏ Ask your peer the following questions about your editorial.

❏ Take notes on what your peer says about how you can improve your draft. Remind your peer to give you specific examples from your draft.

❏ After you have completed this form, use a colored pencil to make necessary revisions based on your peer's comments.

1. Does the beginning of my editorial grab your attention? Why or why not?_____

_____

_____

_____

2. What is the topic that I am writing about? _____

_____

_____

_____

3. What is my opinion on the topic? What words do I use to indicate my opinion? _____

_____

_____

_____

4. What two details do I use to support my opinion?

   a. _____

   b. _____

5. How could I improve my conclusion?_____

_____

_____

Rubric for an Editorial

Writer: _____ Date: _____

Directions: Use the following rubric to evaluate your editorial.

	Self	Peer	Teacher
Content			
1. A lead (beginning) that grabs the reader's attention. (4)			
2. The writer's opinion on the topic is clearly stated. (2)			
3. The writer has provided at least two supporting details for his/her opinion. (2)			
4. The conclusion summarizes the key ideas of the editorial. (2)			
Mechanics			
1. Correct paragraphing (3)			
2. Spelling (2)			
Total out of 15 points			

Writer's Evaluation

1. What are your strengths in this editorial? _____

_____

_____

_____

_____

2. What do you plan to do to improve your editorial? _____

_____

_____

_____

_____

Using Graphic Organizers

Objective: The student will use graphic organizers to brainstorm ideas for an editorial.

Procedure

1. Identify for students four different kinds of graphic organizers that can help them plan their editorials: compare/contrast, sequence chain, problem/solution chart, and web. Show them each of the graphic organizers and explain that authors use graphic organizers to plan their writing.

2. Read the sample editorial on page 45 or 46 and ask students to use the appropriate graphic organizer to deconstruct the author's writing on the overhead.

3. Brainstorm with the students topics for their own articles. Possible topics include sports, friends, social issues, current events, and the environment.

4. Have students do research on their topics and then use one of the graphic organizers to plan their writing.

5. Use any of the graphic organizers in science or social studies classes to organize written reports.

Portfolio Piece: Instruct students to include their graphic organizers and rough drafts of the editorials in their portfolios as an example of the writing process. Have them each write a reflection about the benefits of using a graphic organizer.

Publishing: Create a bulletin board of the students' graphic organizers. Share graphic organizers and discuss the benefits of using a graphic organizer.

Technology Connection: Create original graphic organizers using the computer program "Student Writing Center."

Home-School Connection: Have students use a web with a family member to brainstorm possibilities for a weekend activity. Instruct the students to discuss the pros and cons of each item on the web with the family member and use the web as a tool to make a final decision.

Assessment: Assess the students' abilities to choose the appropriate graphic organizers to plan their editorials. Evaluate the students' abilities to use the brainstorming on the graphic organizers to organize their editorials.

Graphic Organizer #1:
Web

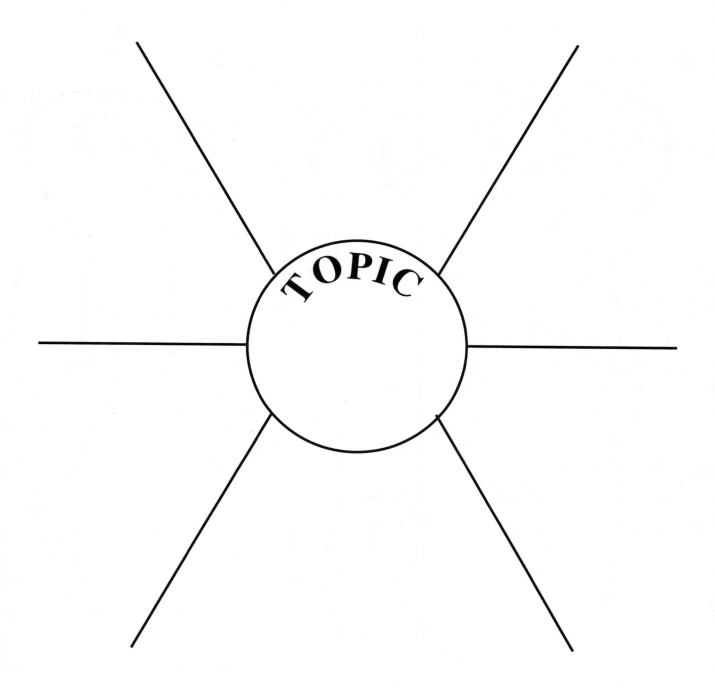

Graphic Organizer #2: Compare and Contrast

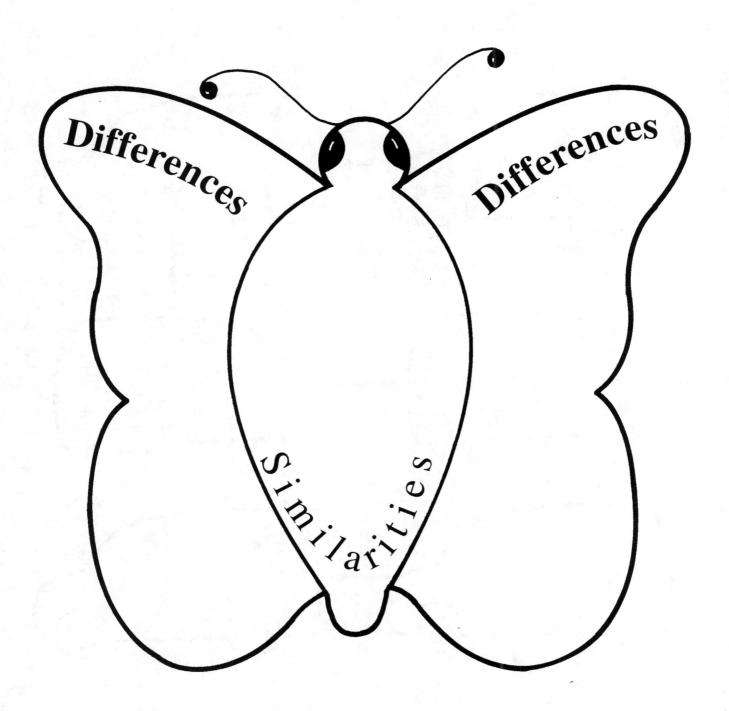

Graphic Organizer #3:
Sequence Chain

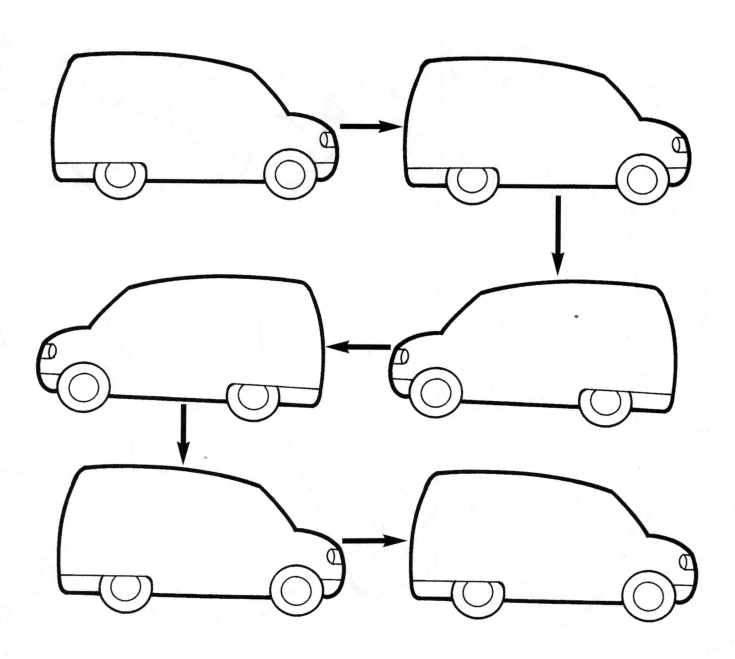

Graphic Organizer #4:
Problem/Solution Chart

Problem

Proposed Solution

Pros	Cons

Final Solution

Conducting Research

Objectives: The student will read the newspaper's editorial section to find many opinions on the same topic. The student will research different opinions on a topic of personal choice in the library.

Procedure

1. Pass out copies of a newspaper and have students turn to the "letters to the editor" section. Read the letters and discuss the readers' varying opinions on one topic.

2. Assist students in constructing research questions. Examples: "Should humans develop a colony on Mars?" "Should trees be cleared from a plot of land to build a large mall?" "Do we need more technology in schools?" "Is the United States doing a good job of protecting endangered species?"

3. Have students complete the "Yes/No" reproducible on page 55. Take students to the library and allow them time to answer their research questions. Remind them to record their sources on the reproducible.

4. Have students work in pairs to do their research. One partner can research the "Yes" opinion on the topic, and the other partner can research the "No" opinion on the topic.

5. Divide the students into different pairs and have them switch papers. Have them read each other's editorials and write a letter to one another agreeing or disagreeing with the opinion of their partners.

Portfolio Piece: Instruct students to each include the "Yes/No" worksheet in the portfolio and write a reflection on the ease or difficulty with which they found the opposing opinions connected to their research questions.

Publishing: Have students create cartoons that represent the opposing opinions on their topic. Create a colorful bulletin board of the cartoons and post the words "Yes" and "No" throughout the display.

Technology Connection: Instruct the students to research multiple points of view on the Internet. Show students how to select keywords to research their questions, using search engines like *Yahoo!*, *Excite*, or *Infoseek*.

Home-School Connection: Have students read the "letters to the editor" in a publication that the family receives. Instruct the students and family members to take sides and agree or disagree with the various letters and provide support for their opinions.

Assessment: Evaluate the students' abilities to find at least two "yes" opinions and two "no" opinions related to their research topics. Also, evaluate the students' abilities to record the sources from which they got their information.

Yes/No Worksheet

Directions: Use this worksheet to gather different opinions on your topic from a variety of sources. After you record an opinion in either the "Yes" or "No" column, remember to record the title of the book or magazine in which you found the information. Include the page and paragraph numbers on which the information was found.

Topic: _____

Audience: _____

Purpose: _____

Research Question: _____

_____

Yes	No
Information: **Source:**	**Information:** **Source:**
Information: **Source:**	**Information:** **Source:**
Information: **Source:**	**Information:** **Source:**

Standards and Benchmarks: 1A, 1D, 4A, 4B, 4C, 4F

Choosing Reliable Sources

Objective: The student will identify and use reliable sources when writing editorials.

Procedure

1. Read "Little Red Riding Hood" to the students. After reading, ask the students, "If the wolf asked you to take a walk in the woods with him because he wanted to show you a surprise, would you?" Discuss the students' responses and then introduce them to the word "reliable." *Reliable* means information or a person that can be trusted. Students should recognize that the wolf was not reliable because he could not be trusted.

2. Inform the students that a "source" is a place where you find information. Reinforce for the students that a "reliable source" is information that can be trusted.

3. Read an editorial from a newspaper and identify the author's topic and purpose. Discuss the sources cited in the article. Write the sources on the board. (If there aren't any sources identified in the article, have the students guess where the author got the information.)

4. Instruct the students to use one of the graphic organizers on pages 50–53 to brainstorm a topic for an editorial.

5. Discuss different sources of information for finding out more about their topic (Examples: encyclopedias, dictionaries, newspapers, magazines, books, Internet sites, interviews with experts, etc.).

6. Discuss with the students the importance of choosing reliable sources. Ways to verify the reliability of the sources include the following:

   • Check the publishing company. Well-known publishing companies care about maintaining their reputations.

   • Read to find out if the information can be confirmed in at least two sources.

   • Check out the author, his/her reputation, and possible reasons for writing the information.

7. Have the students write an editorial and research information. Instruct them to use the reproducible "Choosing Reliable Sources" to guide them.

Portfolio Piece: Instruct the students to include their editorials in their portfolios and defend each of the sources that they used. Then, have students each write a reflection in order to answer the question, "Did you use reliable sources?" Students will need to use examples from sources to support their answers to this question.

Publishing: Post editorials on the school's Web site.

Technology Connection: Use the Internet to research an issue. Confirm the reliability of the information in at least one print source (newspaper, magazine, or book.) Use a word-processing program to add, delete, move, and remove portions of the editorial to ensure that all information is organized.

Home-School Connection: Instruct students to watch a favorite TV show with a family member and discuss the commercials in the show for reliability of information.

Assessment: Evaluate the students' ability to complete the reproducible.

Choosing Reliable Sources *(cont.)*

Directions: As you find information, use the following guidelines to evaluate whether or not the information is reliable.

❑ Check the publishing company. Is it a well-known company?

❑ Read to make sure the information can be confirmed in at least two other sources.

❑ Check out the author. Is the author well-known? What are the author's reasons for writing the information?

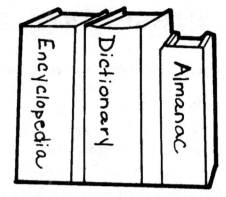

Information	Steps taken to check reliability of information	Is the information reliable? (Yes or No)

Standards and Benchmarks: 1A, 1D, 1E, 1F, 1J, 4B, 4D

Presenting Two Sides of an Issue

Objective: The student will write editorials that present two or more sides of an issue in order to present a balanced argument.

Procedure

1. Read aloud the first two paragraphs of the "Example of an Editorial About a School Issue" on page 46 and identify the author's topic, audience, purpose, and opinion on the issue.

2. After the second paragraph, use the "Presenting Two Sides of an Issue" reproducible as an overhead to identify the topic, audience, and purpose of the article. Assist the students in identifying the author's opinion and the "opposite side" of the issue.

3. Ask the students, "What questions do you have about the opposite side of the issue?" "Does the author answer these questions within the text of the editorial?" Instruct the students to point to specific examples from the text to support their answers.

4. Discuss any questions that the author did not answer. Ask the students, "Why did the author not address these questions?"

5. Have students write their own editorials that address two sides of an issue. Instruct them to use the reproducible entitled "Presenting Two Sides of an Issue" to help anticipate the readers' questions.

6. Brainstorm a number of issues and have students go to the library to research both sides. Students can use encyclopedias and do keyword searches on the Internet.

Portfolio Piece: Instruct the students to include their editorials in their portfolios and highlight with different colors both sides of the issue that they addressed. Then, have students each write a reflection in answer to the question, "Did you present a balanced argument?" Students will need to use examples from their editorials in support.

Publishing: Send the editorials to the publisher of a local newspaper for publication.

Technology Connection: In a word-processing program, set up columns. In each column, write the key points to each side of the issue. Use this brainstorming to write a balanced argument.

Home-School Connection: Read editorials in magazines and newspapers and identify both sides of the issues.

Assessment: Evaluate the students' completion of the worksheet entitled "Two Sides of the Issue." Encourage students to think of at least two questions and two responses for the chart designed to anticipate reader's questions.

Presenting Two Sides of an Issue *(cont.)*

Directions: Identify the following parts of your editorial. Then predict and answer the questions that your reader may have concerning the opposing viewpoint.

Topic (Issue): _____

Audience: _____

Purpose: _____

Author's Opinion on the Issue: _____

_____

_____

The Opposite Opinion on the Issue: _____

_____

_____

Questions About the Opposing Viewpoint	Author's Response to the Questions

Interviewing

Objective: The student will use interviewing skills to gather information from an expert on a topic for an editorial.

Procedure

1. Inform the students that they may need to interview an expert in order to gain information about the topics for their editorials.

2. Have students identify their topics. Then, have them brainstorm possible "experts" who would have more information on the topics. For example, if students were going to write about nutritional lunches during school, then they may want to interview the school cafeteria manager and the school nurse.

3. Distribute the "Interview Worksheet" and review the questions with the students. Have the students brainstorm any other questions they would like to ask the "expert" and write those questions on the back of the worksheet.

4. Divide the students into pairs and have them practice their interviewing skills. Inform them that good interviewers complete the following steps:

   - They come to the interview prepared with questions.
   - They listen attentively to the interviewee's answer.
   - They take notes during the interview.
   - They plan follow-up questions.

5. Students should arrange with their "experts" a time for an interview. Students should take notes on their interview worksheets.

6. Divide students into pairs and have one student take on the persona of the author of a book and the other student be the reader. Have the "reader" interview the "author" about various literary elements in the book.

Portfolio Piece: Have students each write a reflection in which they identify the most effective question that they asked in the interview. Also, have students identify their strengths and weaknesses as interviewers.

Publishing: On a bulletin board, post students' "Interview Sheets" alongside their editorials that incorporate the interview information. Have students highlight the interview information in their editorials.

Technology Connection: Have students conduct an online interview using a tool such as *Yahoo! Instant Messenger.*

Home-School Connection: Have students interview a family member about his/her job. Inform the students that they should specifically practice their listening and notetaking skills in this exercise.

Assessment: Evaluate students' interview worksheets for completeness and evaluate the students' ability to incorporate the interview information into their editorials.

Interview Worksheet

Directions: Use the following worksheet to interview an expert on the topic about which you will be writing your editorial.

Topic: _____

1. What is your position? _____

   _____

   _____

2. What do you know about the topic?_____

   _____

   _____

   _____

3. How did you learn this information?_____

   _____

   _____

   _____

4. Could you show me an example or tell me a story to illustrate what you know about the topic? _____

   _____

   _____

   _____

5. What will my audience need to know about this topic? _____

   _____

   _____

   _____

   _____

6. Who else could I interview to find out more information about this topic?_____

   _____

Classifying Fact and Opinion

Objective: The student will use fact and opinion to support an opinion and meet the needs of the intended audience.

Procedure

1. On the chalkboard or overhead, define fact and opinion for the students: A fact is something that can be proven. An *opinion* conveys thoughts, feelings, or ideas that cannot be proven.

2. Distribute the reproducible entitled "Classifying Fact and Opinion." Instruct students to fill in the worksheet as they listen to the "Example of an Editorial About a School Issue" on page 46. Pause throughout the reading and discuss with the students those parts of the text that fall into the categories of fact or opinion.

3. After reading the editorial, discuss the worksheet with the students. Use the following questions: Does the author use mostly facts, mostly opinions, or a balance of each? How could the author use facts and/or opinions differently in order to better persuade the reader?

4. Read the "Example of a Business Letter" on page 13. Identify the facts and opinions in this letter. You may want to have the students identify facts and opinions with different-colored highlighters or colored pencils. Discuss the questions in #3 above.

5. Partner students and have them evaluate each other's use of fact and opinion.

6. Read the "Example of a Personal Letter" on page 23 and have the students identify all of the opinions contained therein.

Portfolio Piece: Have the students each write their own editorials and then write reflections in which they identify the facts and opinions included in their editorials. Have them reflect on the importance of including a balance of both in their writing in order to affect the reader.

Publishing: Create a bulletin board with the definitions of the words *fact* and *opinion*. Under each definition publish examples from student editorials. For added fun, create a bulletin board that is interactive and have the students sort the examples into fact and opinion as an enrichment activity. Periodically replace the examples with new examples.

Technology Connection: Have students post their magazine and their editorials on the school's Web site. Using a word-processing program, have the students replace all of the opinions in their editorials with facts and save the document with a new file name. Have the students decide which editorial is better: the one with facts and opinions or the one with facts only.

Home-School Connection: Instruct students to look through books (fiction, nonfiction, and reference) and magazines at home to find examples of fact and opinion.

Assessment: Determine if mastery has been achieved by reading the students' "Classifying Fact and Opinion" worksheets and evaluating whether they have completed the prompts and chart correctly.

Classifying Fact and Opinion *(cont.)*

Directions: Use this worksheet to evaluate a piece of writing for fact and opinion. You may use this worksheet to evaluate other people's writing or your own writing.

Remember: A *fact* is something that can be proven. An *opinion* conveys thoughts, feelings, or ideas that cannot be proven.

Topic: _____

Audience: _____

Purpose: _____

_____

Author's opinion on the topic (issue): _____

_____

Examples of Facts	Examples of Opinions

Audience in Editorial Writing

Objective: The student will use knowledge of the audience to appeal to the audience's emotions and interests in order to be persuasive.

Procedure

1. Ask the students who the audience is for an editorial published in a magazine. Students should respond that the audience is the readership for that magazine.

2. Read aloud the reproducible entitled "Audience-Analysis Guide for Editorials." Instruct the students to keep these questions in mind as they read the "Example of an Editorial About a School Issue."

3. Read the editorial on page 46 and pause throughout the reading to discuss the clues the author gives about knowledge of the audience.

4. Have students complete the "Audience-Analysis Guide for Editorials" in response to the school issue editorial. Encourage students to answer all of the questions by making inferences. Remind the students to draw on their own lives and personal experiences since they are part of the intended audience.

5. Ask the students to find specific places in the text of the editorial that show that the author is using his/her knowledge of the audience.

6. Have students select a topic about which to write an editorial. Have them complete the "Audience-Analysis Guide" to gather information about their audience.

7. Read articles, poems, and stories and analyze the authors' appeals to the audience.

Portfolio Piece: Have students identify their strengths and weaknesses in using their knowledge of the audience to write their editorials.

Publishing: Create a bulletin board and post the students' analyses along with a picture that shows what the audience looks like. Students should create illustrations or cut pictures out of a magazine to represent the gender, age, education, and socio-economic status of the audience.

Technology Connection: Have students read articles online and complete the "Audience-Analysis Guide for Editorials." Ask the question, "What assumptions do online authors make about the audience that are different from those of authors of articles, stories, poems that are not online?"

Home-School Connection: Instruct students to discuss with a family member billboards and other advertisements that they see in everyday life. Have students identify the assumptions that the ad and billboard creators are making about their audiences.

Assessment: Evaluate students' abilities to respond to each of the items listed on the audience reproducible with accuracy and insight.

Audience-Analysis Guide for Editorials

Directions: Competent writers always have a "picture" in their minds of their intended audience. If you think about the audience before you write, you will be better able to write an editorial that meets the audience's needs. Respond to the following questions in order to get to know the audience.

Remember: When you are writing an editorial, the audience is the readership of your magazine, newspaper, or newsletter.

Tip: There may be multiple answers for each question.

1. What is the age group and gender of the intended audience? _____
   _____

2. What is the highest level of education of the audience? _____

3. What is the audience's "job"? _____
   _____

4. Where does the audience live? (city, rural, suburban, house, apartment, etc.) _____
   _____

5. What are the audience's interests? _____
   _____
   _____

6. What are the audience's beliefs? _____
   _____
   _____

7. What is the audience's greatest priority? _____
   _____

8. What makes the audience cry? _____
   _____
   _____

9. What makes the audience laugh? _____
   _____
   _____

10. What does the audience already know about the topic? _____
    _____
    _____

Standards and Benchmarks: 1A, 1B, 1D, 1E, 1F, 1J

Leads

Objective: The student will write a lead that develops the readers' interest and introduces the topic of the editorial.

Procedure

1. Write the definition of a lead on the chalkboard or overhead: A *lead* is the way the author starts the text. Leads must "grab" the reader and entice him/her to read on.

2. Read aloud the "Example of an Editorial About a Community Issue" on page 45. Discuss with the students the following questions, "Does the lead of this editorial grab your attention? Why or why not? What words or phrases help develop your interest? What is the topic of this editorial?"

3. Display the reproducible entitled "Kinds of Leads for Starting an Editorial." This reproducible includes the best methods for writing editorial leads with an example for each method.

4. Pass out copies of newspapers. Have students choose one of the editorials from a magazine, identify the lead, and write an alternative lead. Have them discuss with a partner which lead best suits the topic and purpose of the article.

5. Create a matching game for students. Find many examples of leads in magazines, newspapers, and stories. Cut the leads out and laminate them. Put each of the types of leads on colored construction paper. Divide the students into groups of four. Have them match the types of leads with the examples of leads.

Portfolio Piece: Have students write leads to be included in their portfolios. Ask students to also write a reflection explaining how the kind of lead they chose will grab their reader's interest and make him/her want to read further. Students should select particular words and phrases that they feel will be particularly appealing to the reader.

Publishing: Have the students share their leads with the class. Create an interactive bulletin board with student samples of each kind of lead posted on the board. Make a folder of sentence strips identifying each kind of lead. Students can match the kind of lead with the student example.

Technology Connection: Have students use a word-processing program to write their leads. Encourage students to use spell checking and grammar checking.

Home-School Connection: Have students read a magazine editorial, highlight the lead, and discuss the method used with a family member.

Assessment: Use the rubric for editorials on page 48 to score the students' leads.

Kinds of Leads for Starting an Editorial

Directions: Read the list of methods for writing a lead in Part I. Identify the method used for each of the sample leads in Part II.

Part I: Methods for Writing a Lead

Lead #1—uses a strong visual image

Lead #2—uses dialogue

Lead #3—uses facts and statistics about the topic

Lead #4—uses an emotional anecdote

Lead #5—uses a personal story

Lead #6—uses a rhetorical question

Part II: Sample Leads

Topic: Community Participation	Method
Do the members of our community participate in keeping our neighborhood safe and clean? How can we create a greater commitment to our community?	
Imagine a community where every lawn is cut, the shrubs are nicely trimmed, and all of the flower gardens are mulched and regularly weeded. Imagine houses that are well maintained with freshly painted doors, shutters, and garages. Imagine a neighborhood where dogs and cats are not permitted to roam freely. Imagine taking a walk along the quiet, clean streets and admiring the well-kept houses and lawns.	
"Hey, Leo! Do you want to come over and help me rake my yard this weekend? When we are finished on my yard, then we'll work on yours! Sound like a deal?" asked Tom. "Sure, Tom! I'll be over in 10 minutes with my rake," replied Leo. Does the above scenario reflect your neighborhood? Communities across the nation are struggling with issue of working together to maintain our neighborhoods.	
I remember the time that I was walking through our neighborhood and noticed the house with weeds as high as the second story, trash in the driveway, and toys strewn around the yard. I remember seeing the house with an old red, rusted car abandoned in the driveway and a huge pile of logs that had been sitting in the yard for months.	
Once upon a time, there was a neighborhood in which people played loud music morning, noon, and night. Weeds filled what once were beautiful flower beds, and trash lined the street curbs. One day, people decided that they didn't want to live in this neighborhood anymore, but upon putting their houses up for sale, they soon discovered that no one wanted to move in.	
92% of the residents in the Hometown Community keep their yards and homes in excellent condition. After a house in this community is put on the real estate market, it takes an average of two weeks for the home to sell. Based on these statistics, how important is neighborhood upkeep in the Hometown Community?	

Identifying Voice

Objective: The student will identify the voice of the author of an editorial in order to learn how to find his/her own voice in writing.

Procedure

1. Write the definition of voice on the board: *Voice* is the way the author writes about a subject that reveals his/her personality as well as his/her feelings and thoughts about the subject.

2. On the board or overhead, brainstorm a list of more words that would be helpful in identifying the voice of the author. Examples include *happy, sad, angry, sarcastic, concerned, overjoyed, thankful, appreciative, skeptical, overwhelmed, surprised,* etc.

3. Read the "Example of an Editorial About a School Issue" on page 46 and ask students to listen for the voice of the writer. When you have finished reading, discuss with the students which words or sentences describe the voice of the writer. Use the reproducible entitled "Identifying Voice" to record the students' responses. Discuss with the students how to infer the author's feelings on the subject.

4. Have students write about a recent family vacation. When they are finished, have them highlight or underline words that reveal their feelings about the subject.

5. Have students write a response to the voice they identified in "Example of an Editorial About a School Issue." Have students write about a time when they felt the same as the author. Have them identify the 5 Ws of this memory that connect with the author's feelings.

Portfolio Piece: Instruct students to write an editorial about proper behavior in school. Then have the students highlight or underline all of the words or sentences that reveal their beliefs on the topic. Finally, have the students write a reflection about their strengths and weaknesses in identifying their feelings on the subject.

Publishing: Create a bulletin board of the students' editorials. On bright paper, have the students write a single word that reveals their feelings about the topic that they wrote about in their editorials. Match the words with the students' editorials.

Technology Connection: Have students write e-mail messages to online buddies about books that they are currently reading. Instruct the students to each identify the voice in the e-mail messages pertaining to the buddies' opinions of their books.

Home-School Connection: Have students read editorials in magazines and newspapers and discuss with their parents the effect that voice has upon the reader.

Assessment: Evaluate the students' understanding of voice by assessing the completeness and accuracy of the worksheet entitled "Identifying Voice."

Identifying Voice *(cont.)*

Directions: Use the following graphic organizer to analyze the author's voice. You may use this graphic organizer to analyze your own writing.

Remember: *Voice* is the way the author writes about a subject that reveals his/her personality, as well as his/her feelings about the subject.

Topic: _____

Audience: _____

Purpose: _____

_____

_____

Words, Sentence, or Passage from the Article or Letter	Feelings on the Topic

Standards and Benchmarks: 1A, 1B, 1D, 1G, 1J, 1K, 4B, 4D, 4F

Identifying and Supporting an Opinion

Objective: The student will write an opinion statement, support the opinion with detailed evidence, and cite sources of information correctly.

Procedure

1. On the chalkboard or overhead, define the word *opinion* for the students. In editorial writing, an opinion is the author's belief about the subject.

2. Read aloud the "Example of an Editorial About a Community Issue" on page 45. As they listen, students should be able to identify the topic, audience, purpose, opinion, and supporting reasons.

3. Present the students with the following topic: school lunch. Have the students create an opinion statement pertaining to the topic, such as: It is important that school lunches be nutritious.

4. Discuss with the students what they would need to do in order to find supporting details for their opinion statement on school lunch. Students should understand that they will need to do research to support their opinions. Students can read books, magazines, pamphlets, brochures, encyclopedias, and Web sites in order to find information to support their opinions.

5. Have students complete the reproducible entitled "Identifying and Supporting an Opinion" on page 71. Guide students when writing the reasons in support of their stance. Remind them that reasons can include well-known facts, examples from personal experience, logical reasons, examples from text, and expert opinions.

6. Take students to the school library to research their topic. Encourage students to use key word searches to find information in encyclopedias, indexes, almanacs, and on the Internet.

Portfolio Piece: Have students use their "Identifying and Supporting an Opinion" worksheets to write an editorial. Have the students write reflections that identify their most powerful piece of evidence.

Publishing: Have students write their opinion statements about school-related issues on sentence strips. Publish the sentence strips in a school showcase. Plan a community service project that allows the students to take action on their opinions.

Technology Connection: Use a digital camera to take pictures of the students taking action to solve community issues. Post pictures and editorials in the school showcase.

Home-School Connection: Instruct students to interview or survey their parents and neighbors about school-related issues.

Assessment: Evaluate the students editorial essays specifically for the skill of identifying and supporting an opinion.

Identifying and Supporting an Opinion *(cont.)*

Directions: Identify your opinion and the supporting details for your opinion in the worksheet below. The stronger your details and evidence are, the more persuasive your letter will be.

Remember: When you state your opinion, you are giving your beliefs about a particular topic or issue. Make sure that your opinion statement is simple, clear, and specific.

Author's opinion statement: _____

_____

_____

Supporting details for your opinion may include well-known facts, examples from personal experience, logical reasons, examples from text, or expert opinion (gained through research or interviews).

Supporting Details	Source

Citing Sources of Information

Objective: The student will cite various sources of information for the purpose of correctly attributing text to authors.

Procedure

1. Have students determine the topic about which they want to write an editorial.

2. Take the students to the school library and preview the sources of information that are available to them. Ask the school librarian to describe magazine subscriptions, encyclopedias, almanacs, historical atlases, books, pamphlets, brochures, ERIC, Facts on File, and various other resource materials for the students.

3. As the students gather information on their "Identifying and Supporting an Opinion" worksheet on page 71, also have them record their sources on the reproducible entitled "Citing Sources of Information."

4. Circulate around the room and offer guidance as needed to the students.

5. Divide the students into pairs and have them divide the research tasks. One student can work on gathering information while the other student can cite the resources. After students have finished gathering information and recording their sources, have them alphabetize their lists by authors' last names. Inform the students that the worksheet "Citing Sources of Information" requires them to record author, title, and year, which is the foundation for learning how to write a full biography in MLA or AP style.

Portfolio Piece: Have the students include their "Citing Sources" worksheets in their portfolios and have them each write a reflection in which they identify the importance of citing sources of information correctly. Students should recognize that this skill is important in order to appropriately recognize and attribute the work of authors. Inform the students that they would want the same respect towards their work as authors.

Publishing: Create a bulletin board display that has a picture of a woman with a telescope gazing at students' "Citing Sources of Information" worksheets. Title the bulletin board "A Sighting of Citings!"

Technology Connection: Instruct the students to visit a Web site that contains rules and models for correct MLA and AP style. Ask students what they would have to add to their worksheets in order to make the information conform to MLA style.

Home-School Connection: Over the course of a week, instruct the students to read magazine articles, newspaper articles, short stories, and children's books of their choice with a family member. Have the students complete their "Citing Sources of Information" worksheets with a family member and discuss the importance of correctly recognizing an author's work.

Assessment: Evaluate the students' ability to correctly and accurately complete the worksheet "Citing Sources of Information."

Citing Sources of Information *(cont.)*

Directions: Use the following chart to record the author, title, and year of sources (magazine articles, books, stories, newspaper articles, pamphlets, brochures) of information that you find to support your opinion.

Author	Title	Year

Order of Importance

Objective: The student will identify an issue of importance and organize the key points in order to make the most powerful argument to the audience.

Procedure

1. Have students identify three home issues about which they feel strongly. Examples might include bedtime, amount of TV watching, phone privileges, meals, etc.

2. Distribute the reproducible entitled "Order of Importance." Instruct the students to choose one home issue, create an opinion statement, and at least three key points that support their opinion. Example of an opinion statement: I think I should be able to go to bed each evening at 9:00 P.M. instead of 8:00 P.M. Key points: (1) I will have more time to read before bed, (2) I will have more time to clean up my room before bed, and (3) I will have more time to lay out my clothes the night before school.

3. Use a student example or the example written above to model for the students how to put the key points in order. Inform the students that they should each determine their most important point, the point that will make the most impact on the audience. That point should either be first or last, depending on where the author wants to create emphasis. Discuss with the students the pros and cons of each approach. Putting the most important point first will grab the reader from the beginning. Putting the most important point last will leave the reader with the most important point fresh in mind.

4. Have the students rank their key points on their reproducible. Have them share responses with a partner and gather feedback from peers on the strengths and weaknesses of their different approaches.

Portfolio Connection: Instruct students to write a reflection in which they explain the order of their key points and the rationale for their organization.

Publishing: Create a bulletin board of the students' editorials and post next to the editorial the students' explanations for how they ranked the key points of their editorials.

Technology Connection: Have students use the bulleting function to number their key points. Then, have all the students use the cut and paste function to arrange their key points in the order that is most persuasive to the audience.

Home-School Connection: Instruct the students to find editorials in newspapers at home and discuss with a family member the author's choices when ordering the key points.

Assessment: Use the rubric for editorials on page 48 and evaluate the students' abilities to order their key points in a way that appeals to the audience in the most effective way.

Order of Importance *(cont.)*

Directions: Use this worksheet to organize the key points of your editorial.

Topic: _____

Audience: _____

Purpose: _____

_____

Opinion: I believe/do not believe that . . . _____

_____

_____

Key Points to Support My Opinion	Order

What is your most important point? Why? Where did you put this point—first or last? _____

_____

_____

_____

Linking Your Ideas Using Transitions

Objective: The student will use transitions to link ideas between paragraphs in editorial writing.

Procedure

1. Inform the students that they need to link the ideas between their paragraphs with transitions. Write the following transitions on the board for order of importance: *first*, *second*, *third*, *next*, *additionally*, *also*, *last*, *finally*, *therefore*, *however*, and *similarly*.

2. Have students use their worksheets from the previous lesson on "Order of Importance" to complete the worksheet entitled "Linking Your Ideas Using Transitions." Have students put their key points in order and choose an appropriate transition to link each new idea to the next.

3. Instruct students to draft their editorials using the transition worksheet.

4. When the students are finished drafting their worksheets, have them highlight each of the transitions that they used. If they can't highlight any transitions, have them go back and add appropriate transitions.

5. Provide the students with a series of paragraphs that do not have any transitions. Next, give students transitions written on separate sentence strips. In groups of two, have them decide which transitions appropriately link the ideas between the paragraphs they were given.

Portfolio Piece: Have students include their editorials in their portfolios with the transitions highlighted. Have students each write a reflection on how they chose appropriate transitions to link several related paragraphs.

Publishing: Create a bulletin board which includes the students' editorials with transitions highlighted and sentence strips with the transitions attractively interspersed between and among the student editorials.

Technology Connection: Have students experiment with the thesaurus function in a word-processing program in order to come up with alternatives to the transitions they have already selected.

Home-School Connection: Have students each read three articles with a family member and keep a running list of transitions that link paragraphs. Instruct the students to post the lists next to their desks at home to use as references when trying to think of transitions.

Assessment: Evaluate the students' ability to complete the worksheet "Linking Your Ideas Using Transitions." Read the students' editorials and evaluate their appropriate use of transitions within their editorials.

Linking Your Ideas Using Transitions *(cont.)*

Directions: Complete the following worksheet in order to help you to link your key points using transitions. Write the key point of each of your paragraphs in the left-hand column. In the right-hand column, write the best transition word to link your key points.

Transitions for Order of Importance

first, second, third, next, additionally, also, last, finally, therefore, however, similarly

---

Opinion Statement: _____

_____

Transition	Key Points
	Paragraph 1 of the body:
	Paragraph 2 of the body:
	Paragraph 3 of the body:

Word Choice for Persuasive Writing

Objective: The student will use precise, unemotional language in editorial writing in order to present their arguments logically.

Procedure

1. Present the students with the following guidelines for using persuasive language:

    Persuasive language . . .
    - is calm and reasonable.
    - includes reasons and specific examples.
    - avoids exaggerations and words that show strong emotions such as anger.
    - avoids bias and insults.

2. Distribute the reproducible entitled "Word Choice for Persuasive Writing." Read the examples of persuasive writing in Part I. Ask the students: Does this example use precise, controlled, unemotional language? How do you know? Discuss the students' responses.

3. Read "Example of an Editorial About a School Issue" and ask the students to listen for precise, controlled language. After reading the editorial, use the following questions to guide the discussion:
    - ❏ Is the language calm and reasonable?
    - ❏ What specific examples support the author's key ideas?
    - ❏ Are there exaggerations, biased statements, or examples of anger?

4. Complete Part II of the reproducible. Identify words and/or phrases that show reason and control; identify any words and/or phrases that show bias or strong emotions.

5. Have students write their own editorials and analyze them for controlled, precise, unemotional language. Divide students into pairs and have them read each other's editorials and analyze them, using the same criteria.

Portfolio Piece: Have the students highlight the precise, controlled language in their editorials. Have them each write a reflection in which they predict how their use of language will affect the reader.

Publishing: Have the students create a word list of precise, controlled vocabulary words and a word list of biased, overly emotional words. Post the word lists in the classroom and have the students refer to the lists when they are writing their editorials.

Technology Connection: Use a word-processing program to edit and revise for precise, controlled language. Encourage the students to use the computer thesaurus.

Home-School Connection: Have students role-play a scenario with a family member in which they have to use calm, reasonable language. Discuss with the students their observations after acting out the scenario.

Assessment: Evaluate the students' use of controlled, precise language by reading their editorials and looking for unemotional language. Also, evaluate the students' "Word Choice" worksheets for completeness and accuracy.

Word Choice for Persuasive Writing *(cont.)*

Persuasive language . . .

- is calm and reasonable

- includes reasons and specific examples

- avoids exaggerations, words that show strong emotions, bias, anger, and insults.

Part I

Directions: Read the examples of persuasive writing below and identify whether or not the examples are specific and controlled or biased and overly emotional. Write the words "thumbs up" to identify precise, controlled language and write "thumbs down" to identify biased, highly emotional language.

1. My friend Dan is very obnoxious. He is never kind, and when I'm around him he always hurts my feelings. He never asks how I am doing, and he always brags about himself. He thinks he's the only person on this planet. I am never going to be friends with him again!

2. I am disappointed about the way my friend Dan acts sometimes. When we get together to play after school, he usually talks about himself. For example, yesterday he spent an hour talking about how he hit a home run at his Little League game. When I try to tell him about my sports team, he usually cuts me off to tell a story of his own. It is difficult to be friends with Dan. I think I am going to tell him how I feel and see what he says.

Part II

Directions: Read or listen to an article and complete the chart below.

Examples of Controlled, Precise Language	Examples of Overly Emotional Language

Building Style in Editorial Writing

Objective: The student will write a paragraph using a particular element of style in order to appeal to the audience.

Procedure

1. Write the following elements of style on the chalkboard: rhetorical questions, "imagine that" sentence beginnings, alliteration, similes, and metaphors. Tell the students that using elements of style will make their writing more interesting and appealing to the audience.

2. Read Part I of the "Elements of Style" reproducible to the students. As you read, give the students examples so that they better understand each of the elements.

3. Read the "Example of an Editorial About a School Issue" on page 46 and complete Part II of "Elements." As you read, record elements of style in the chart. Discuss with the students the effects that the elements of style have on their emotions and feelings about the topic the author is discussing.

4. Have students choose one of the elements of style and write a short paragraph using this particular element. Brainstorm with the students topics for their paragraphs. (Sample topics: food, weather, pets, shopping, the environment, science, education, toys, clothes, characters, etc.) If necessary share with them this example: Imagine a huge snowstorm arrived in your town unexpectedly. White, cold snow crystals swirled everywhere, creating poor visibility on the roadways. Would you be prepared? (Elements of style used: "imagine that," imagery, and rhetorical question.)

5. Divide students into pairs and have the students read each other's paragraphs. Have students make sure that they have at least two elements of style in their paragraphs.

6. Read articles in magazines and have students look for elements of style. Have the students use the reproducible entitled "Elements of Style" to record examples.

Portfolio Piece: Have students include two elements of style in their editorials and each write a reflection in which they identify the ease or difficulty with which they were able to incorporate the elements of style.

Publishing: Have students each share their best original stylistic element with the class in round-robin fashion.

Technology Connection: Have students use a word-processing program to revise their paragraphs by adding and deleting elements of style, as necessary.

Home-School Connection: Have students read a children's book with a family member and identify and discuss any elements of style they encounter.

Assessment: Evaluate the students' understanding of elements of style by reading and assessing their accurate completion of the "Elements of Style" worksheet.

Elements of Style

Part I

Directions: Read the chart below that contains elements of style. As you read, think about which elements of style you have included in your own writing.

Elements of Style	Definitions and Reasons for Use
Rhetorical question	The author asks a question to get the reader thinking about personal experiences related to the topic and questions/thoughts that the reader has about the topic. "Rhetorical" means that the author doesn't really expect the reader to answer the question.
"Imagine that . . ." sentence beginning	The author uses an "imagine that . . ." sentence beginning to spark the reader's imagination with images and thoughts related to the topic. Often the writer also uses sensory details within the "imagine that . . ." scenario to connect with the reader's thoughts and ideas.
Imagery	The author uses words and phrases to appeal to the reader's five senses. The author uses imagery to appeal to the reader's imagination and help him/her create a picture in his/her mind.
Alliteration	The author uses the same letter to begin two or more words in a series. Authors use alliteration to create emphasis around a particular topic.
Metaphors	Metaphors make implied comparisons between two seemingly dissimilar things which have similar attributes. The author uses metaphors to compare abstract concepts to concrete images so that the concept can be better understood.
Simile	Similes use *like* or *as* to indicate a similarity between two unrelated things. The author uses similes to create interesting pictures in the reader's mind.

Elements of Style *(cont.)*

Part II

Directions: Read the text of the editorial carefully, identify the elements of style used, give an example from the text, and rate the author's use of the element by using the following rating scale:

✓+ = Great!	✓ = OK	✓− = Poor

Element of Style	Example from Text	Rating

Varying Sentence Structure and Length

Objective: The student will vary sentence structure and length in editorial writing in order to improve his/her understanding of style.

Procedure

1. Inform the students of the following definitions: *Sentence structure* is the way that the sentence is built. There are three basic structures: simple, compound, and complex. Authors vary their sentence structure in order to make their writing flow. *Sentence length* is the number of words in the sentence. Authors vary their sentence length in order to create emphasis.

2. Have the students read an article in a magazine. Instruct them to count the words and record the sentence lengths of the first five sentences. Ask the students, "Are any of the sentences the same length?" and "Why wouldn't the author simply make all of the sentences the same length?"

3. In the same article, have the students identify the sentence structure of the second five sentences. Ask the students, "Do any of these sentences have the same structure?" Create a chart on the chalkboard and have the students categorize the sentences into three groups: simple, compound, and complex.

4. Give the students a simple topic (for example, playground, a pet, homework, a sibling). Have the students choose one of these topics and brainstorm sensory details about the topic.

5. Have the students use the details to write a paragraph about their topics. After they have finished their paragraphs, have the students count their sentence lengths. Next, have them identify each of their sentence structures. If the students have sentences that are all about the same length and sentences that are all the same sentence structure, then have the students revise in order to add variety to their style.

Portfolio Piece: Have students include their sensory paragraphs from the above exercise in their portfolios. Instruct them to each write a reflection in which they identify their favorite sentence. Have them identify the length and structure of this sentence and have them explain why they think this sentence will make an impression on the audience.

Publishing: Instruct the students to write a complex sentence about the weather they experienced on the way to school in the morning. Have the students share their sentences in round-robin fashion with the entire class.

Technology Connection: Show students how to use the grammar checking function in a word-processing program to ensure they have avoided sentence fragments and run-ons.

Home-School Connection: Have the students read a short story with a family member and identify the sentence lengths of each of the sentences in the first paragraph.

Assessment: Evaluate the students' accurate completion of "Varying Sentence Structure and Length." Read the students' editorials and determine whether they have applied their knowledge of sentences to their writing.

Varying Sentence Structure and Length *(cont.)*

Directions: Read the text of an editorial carefully and choose three sentences. Copy each of the sentences into the chart and identify the word length and structure for each sentence. Then, as a class discuss the effectiveness of each of the sentences.

Varying Sentence Structure	Authors vary sentence structures to make their writing flow. By using a combination of simple, compound, and complex sentence structures, the minds of the readers more easily follow the arguments of the authors.
Varying Sentence Length	Authors vary sentence lengths to create emphasis. Authors mostly use average and long sentences, but an occasional short sentence creates impact and can have a powerful effect on the reader.

Sentence	Word Length	Structure

Extending Ideas Using Prepositional Phrases

Objective: The student will use prepositional phrases to elaborate on key points and supporting details in editorial writing.

Procedure

1. Ask students to define what it means to elaborate and extend ideas in writing. Ask students to identify ways to extend ideas. Students should respond with the following: using sensory details, adding adjectives, adding similes and metaphors, substituting vivid verbs for boring verbs, and adding prepositional phrases.

2. Distribute the reproducible entitled "Extending Ideas Using Prepositional Phrases." Review with the students the definition of a preposition and examples of prepositions.

3. Have the students complete the "Writer's Practice" section of the reproducible. Circulate around the room and offer guidance as necessary. Consider having the students complete the first four exercises with a partner and the last eight individually.

4. Instruct the students to reread the editorials that they have written and highlight any prepositional phrases that they have already included. Divide students into pairs and have the students work together to identify all of the prepositional phrases.

5. Have the students use colored pencils to add more appropriate prepositional phrases to extend ideas. Model for the students how to do this by making a transparency of one of the student's editorials and adding prepositional phrases as needed for the students to see on the overhead projector.

6. Read a magazine or newspaper article and identify the prepositional phrases.

Portfolio Piece: Have the students each write a reflection in which they identify whether or not the ideas in their editorials are extended enough to meet the needs of the audience.

Publishing: Have the students create a prepositional poem. Give the students a statement (such as "The stone rolled . . .") and have them extend the statement by adding at least four prepositional phrases (e.g., "The stone rolled over the hill, under the bridge, across the road, and into the gully."). Post the poems around the classroom.

Technology Connection: Have the students use a word-processing program to compose their editorials and revise them by adding prepositional phrases as needed.

Home-School Connection: Instruct the students to each describe their school day to a family member by using at least five prepositional phrases.

Assessment: Evaluate the students' ability to accurately complete the 12 exercises in the "Writer's Practice" section of the reproducible. In addition, assess the students' editorials for appropriate use of prepositional phrases in their writing.

Extending Ideas Using Prepositional Phrases *(cont.)*

Directions: Read the information below and then complete the section entitled "Writer's Practice."

A *preposition* is a word that shows the relationship of a noun or pronoun to some other word in a sentence.

Frequently Used Prepositions

about	during	onto
at	except	through
around	for	to
before	from	under
behind	in	with
beneath	into	without
between	of	within
down	on	

Writer's Practice: Circle the prepositional phrase in each sentence. Then write the preposition on the line next to the sentence.

1. The little frog sat under the log. _____

2. The puppy snuggled between the pillows. _____

3. I saw the grocery store around the corner. _____

4. We had to go through the woods to reach grandma's house. _____

5. We laid out the picnic blanket beneath the shady tree. _____

6. I really want you to clean your room before breakfast. _____

7. It is really hard to avoid getting the flu during the school year. _____

8. When the sun came up, there was snow on the ground. _____

9. Today I received a letter from my cousin. _____

10. I will meet you at the mall later tonight. _____

11. I raked all of the leaves. _____

12. Except for a few crumbs, the kitchen is clean. _____

Using End Marks Correctly

Objective: The student's conclusion will connect, summarize, and extend the ideas presented in the body of the editorial.

Procedure

1. Present the following criteria of a conclusion to the students: (1) it begins with a summary statement, (2) it connects the main ideas presented in the body, (3) it connects back to the introduction and the opinion statement, and (4) it connects the ideas in the text to personal experience and events and ideas beyond the text.

2. Have students highlight their opinion statements and main ideas in their editorials. Then have them each write a rough draft of their conclusions, using the "Writing Conclusions" reproducible on page 88 for guidance.

3. Divide the students into pairs and have them read each other's conclusions and check them against the criteria for a conclusion listed at the top of the reproducible entitled "Writing Conclusions." Have students re-draft their conclusions, using their partner's suggestions. Circulate around the room and offer guidance to the students as they write their conclusions.

4. Read an editorial in a local newspaper and use the criteria to discuss the author's conclusion.

Portfolio Piece: Have students write two different conclusions for their editorials. Then, have them select the better one and write a reflection letter in which they identify how they used the conclusion criteria to select the better conclusion.

Publishing: Have students read their conclusions out loud to the class and instruct the student audience to identify the opinion of the author and the supporting details based on the information in the conclusion.

Technology Connection: Have students use a word-processing program to write their editorials. Students can "cut and paste" their opinion statements and key points from the introductions and bodies of their editorials and then revise and rewrite in order to blend the ideas into coherent conclusions.

Home-School Connection: Instruct students to each read a newspaper editorial and discuss how the author summarized the main ideas in the conclusion.

Assessment: Use the rubric for editorials on page 48 to score the students' conclusions. Allow each student to self-evaluate by completing the "Self" portion of the rubric. Allow students to work with peers and complete the "Peer" portion of the rubric. Students should make necessary revisions after this assessment process.

Writing Conclusions

Directions: Use this worksheet to write a complete conclusion that extends your main ideas. Remember that conclusions satisfy the following criteria:

- ❏ They begin with a summary statement.
- ❏ They connect the main ideas presented in the body of your editorial.
- ❏ They connect back to the introduction and your opinion statement.
- ❏ They connect the ideas in the summary to personal experiences or events and ideas beyond the text.

Introduction and Body

Your opinion: _____

_____

Your two or three main ideas from your editorial: _____

_____

_____

_____

Conclusion

Your summary statement: _____

_____

_____

_____

A sentence or two restating your opinion and your main ideas:

_____

_____

_____

A sentence or two that connect the main ideas of your editorial to personal experiences or other information "beyond the text":

_____

_____

_____

Editorial Cartoons

Objective: The student will use editorial cartoons to share a message about a particular school or community issue with the audience.

Procedure

1. Select an editorial cartoon from a newspaper or magazine. Tell the students that editorial cartoons usually focus on a topic that is in the news and are usually only one frame in length. Instruct the students to read the cartoon carefully.

2. Ask students, "What does the cartoonist want the reader to do or think after reading this cartoon?"

3. In groups of four, have the students generate a list of questions they have about the cartoon. After 10 minutes, write some of the students' questions on the board. Discuss the students' questions. Make sure to clarify the humor and sarcasm in the cartoon. Make sure the students understand the topic of the cartoon. Discuss the caption beneath the cartoon.

4. Ask students to read aloud the "Example of an Editorial About a Community Issue" on page 45. Ask the students, "How could we re-create the author's message as an editorial cartoon?" Use the reproducible entitled "Creating an Editorial Cartoon" to identify character(s) and setting.

5. Brainstorm school or community issues and create cartoons.

Portfolio Piece: Instruct the students to include an editorial cartoon in their portfolios. Have them write a reflection in which they identify the topic and purpose of the cartoon. Also, have the students identify whether the author's message is better conveyed through a cartoon or an editorial essay.

Publishing: Have the students place their original cartoons on their desks. Instruct them to stand up and walk around the room for 10 minutes, examining each other's cartoons. Ask students to approach one other student and share a "praise" with that student for his/her cartoon.

Technology Connection: Have the students use a graphics program to create their editorials.

Home-School Connection: Have the students find an editorial cartoon in a magazine or newspaper and discuss with a family member the creator's use of humor and sarcasm.

Assessment: Use the "Rubric for an Editorial Cartoon" on page 91 to evaluate the students' editorial cartoons.

Creating an Editorial Cartoon

Directions: Use the following worksheet to display your editorial cartoon. In the box at the bottom of this page, create an illustration that pokes fun at or points out the humorous side of a serious community or school topic. Include a caption which reveals the purpose of the cartoon.

Topic: _____

Audience: _____

Purpose (What ideas do I want my audience to have after reading this cartoon?): _____

_____

_____

Character(s)	Setting

(caption)

Rubric for an Editorial Cartoon

Cartoon Creator:_____   Date: _____

Directions: Use the following rubric to evaluate your editorial cartoon.

	Self	Peer	Teacher
Completeness			
Topic is clear to the audience (1)			
Topic relates to a current school or community issue that is "hot" (1)			
Message is clear to the audience (1)			
Illustration has characters or settings that enhance the message of the cartoon creator (3)			
Illustrations and caption are neat (1)			
Caption is clearly written and enhances the message of the cartoon (2)			
No spelling errors that interfere with meaning (1)			

Total out of 10 points

Writer's Reflection

What are the strengths in my illustration? _____

_____

_____

_____

What needs to be improved? _____

_____

_____

_____

_____

Planning a Debate

Objective: The student will identify a topic for debate, research both the affirmative and negative opinions on the topic, and then plan and organize the debate's key points.

Procedure

1. Identify as a class a topic for debate and then write the topic in question form on the chalkboard or overhead. For example:

   Topic: Endangered Species

   Debate question: Is the United States taking steps to protect endangered species?

2. Brainstorm with the students a variety of topic questions and write them on the chalkboard or overhead. Examples include "Should human beings colonize Mars?" "Should schools spend more time on service-learning projects?" and "Are people beginning to rely too much on technology?"

3. Divide students into pairs and have them choose one of the class questions or write one of their own. Instruct one student in each partnership to research the "affirmative" (answering the question "yes") and one student to research the "negative" (answering the question "no").

4. Take the students to the library to research their topics and gather facts and examples to support both the affirmative and negative opinions regarding their topics. Have them complete the "Planning a Debate" worksheet. Remind students to use key words, indexes, cross references, and letters on volumes to find information.

5. Inform the students that they will need to study both sides of the topic and prepare to respond to the opposite opinion.

6. Have the students debate, using the information on the reproducible. The student with the affirmative opinion goes first, and the student with the negative opinion follows by responding specifically to the first key point of the argument.

Portfolio Piece: Instruct the students to include their planning worksheets for their debates in their portfolios. Have the students each write a reflection in which they identify the importance of understanding both sides of an issue.

Publishing: Have students perform their debates in front of the class. Have the audience members discuss the effectiveness of each debate and take a side on the issue based on the affirmative and negative opinions presented.

Technology Connection: Have students research their viewpoints online and record the information they find on the "Planning a Debate" worksheet.

Home-School Connection: Instruct students to identify a topic important to the family. Have family members research the topic together and discuss the affirmative and negative viewpoints.

Assessment: Evaluate the students' ability to complete "Planning a Debate."

Planning a Debate (cont.)

Directions: With your partner, research both the affirmative and negative viewpoints of the issue.

Topic: _____

Audience: _____

Topic restated in question form: _____

_____

Research to Support the Affirmative (Yes) Opinion	Research to Support the Negative (No) Opinion

Responding to Prompts for Editorial Writing

Objective: The student will respond to a prompt for editorial writing by stating an opinion on the issue and supporting the opinion with relevant, detailed examples.

Procedure

1. Use the previous lessons in the editorial writing section to teach the students how to develop and organize their editorials and support their opinions with relevant examples. Show students the rubric for editorial writing on page 48 in order to demonstrate how their editorials will be evaluated.

2. Pass out one of the prompts for editorial writing and instruct the students to respond to the corresponding "Quick Write." Students should respond to this question as quickly as possible because it is intended to stimulate their thinking. Tip: Have students brainstorm independently, share their responses with a partner, and then add to their lists based on their discussion.

3. Instruct the students to respond to the prompt. Guide and encourage the students as they are drafting their responses.

4. Have students use the "Peer Response Form for an Editorial" on page 47 to give each other feedback.

5. Instruct the students to revise and re-draft in order to produce a publishable draft.

6. Have the students send their editorials to an editor of a popular children's magazine and ask for feedback. Students could ask for advice on choosing timely topics, selecting relevant support for their opinions, and using enough detail.

Portfolio Piece: Have students respond to many of the prompts and each choose their favorite for inclusion in their portfolios. Have them each write a reflection in which they defend their choices with examples from the text of their editorials.

Publishing: Create a class magazine and have the students rotate in the role of editor. Each week a different student will write an editorial on a timely topic of interest.

Technology Connection: Have students post their editorials on the school's Web site. Create "Webfolios" and have students include their editorials and reflections in their online portfolios.

Home-School Connection: Instruct students to select one of the prompts with a family member and brainstorm possible responses.

Assessment: Use the "Rubric for an Editorial" on page 48 to evaluate the students' editorials.

Prompts for Editorial Writing

Prompt #1: Being Well-Behaved at School Assemblies

Quick Write: Brainstorm three reasons why it is important to be well-behaved at school assemblies.

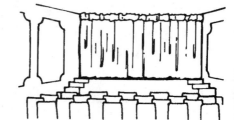

Suppose you and your classmates recently went to see a school assembly featuring reptiles in the auditorium. While you were there, a number of the other students in the auditorium were talking loudly, squirming, and giggling. Write an editorial for your school newspaper in which you request that your classmates be polite and respectful toward the other students in the auditorium and the adults who are presenting the assembly by remaining quiet and still during school performances and presentations. Clearly state your opinion on this issue and include two or three reasons to support your opinion. You may want to consider including the following reasons for requesting a quiet, calm auditorium: respect for others, respect for oneself, showing a good example to younger kids, and maintaining a polite school community. Remember to develop your ideas fully and clearly and to write a strong conclusion summarizing your key points.

Prompt #2: Discouraging Loitering at the Local Fast-Food Restaurant

Quick Write: List three of your favorite fast-food restaurants.

Suppose you and your family went to a local fast food restaurant last Saturday night. While you were in the restaurant, you noticed that there were a number of teenagers loitering outside the restaurant smoking and talking very loudly. Write an editorial and send it to the local high school asking that teenagers not "hang out" in front of fast-food restaurants. Clearly state your opinion on this issue and include two or three reasons to support your opinion. You may consider including the following reasons: respect for other customers of the restaurant; respect for their own health and safety; and maintaining a safe, quiet, and respectful community. Remember to develop your ideas fully and clearly and to write a strong conclusion summarizing your key points.

Prompts for Editorial Writing *(cont.)*

Prompt #3: Donating Clothes and Toys to a Local Charity

Quick Write: List three articles of clothing that you no longer wear and three toys that you no longer play with.

Suppose you read an advertisement from a local charity requesting a donation of clothes and toys. Write an editorial for your school newspaper in which you request that your classmates donate clothes and toys to the charity. Clearly state your opinion on this issue and include two or three reasons to support your opinion. You may want to consider including the following reasons for your request: donations will help clothe and entertain less fortunate children; making a donation will provide motivation for cleaning out cluttered closets; making a donation will help readers feel that they are contributing to the community; and making a donation will show a positive example to younger children. Remember to develop your ideas fully and clearly and to write a strong conclusion summarizing your key points.

Prompt #4: Teaching Foreign Language in Elementary School

Quick Write: List three languages that would be fun to learn.

Suppose you and your classmates decide that you would like to learn a foreign language. Write an editorial in which you request that foreign languages (such as Spanish, French, and Italian) be offered at your school. Clearly state your opinion on this issue and include two or three reasons to support your opinion. You may consider including the following reasons: learning a foreign language helps students know their own language better; according to research, learning a foreign language is easier at a younger age; and learning a foreign language helps you to better understand cultures from around the world. Remember to develop your ideas fully and clearly and to write a strong conclusion summarizing your key points.

Prompts for Editorial Writing *(cont.)*

Prompt #5: Being Quiet During a Fire Drill

Quick Write: Make a list of three things you have to do during a fire drill.

Suppose you and your classmates have to evacuate the school building during a routine fire drill. During the drill, you notice that your classmates are very noisy. Write an editorial for your school newspaper in which you request that your classmates be quiet and orderly during fire drills. Clearly state your opinion on this issue and include two or three reasons to support your opinion. You may want to consider including the following reasons for requesting a quiet, orderly fire drill: kids need to be able to hear their teachers' directions in order to be safe; older kids need to provide a good example to younger kids; and teachers will be impressed with the responsibility of quiet kids and give them more privileges during the regular school day. Remember to develop your ideas fully and clearly and to write a strong conclusion summarizing your key points.

Prompt #6: Promoting Smoke-Free Restaurants

Quick Write: List three reasons why people shouldn't smoke where others are eating.

Suppose you and your family went to a local restaurant last Friday night. While you were eating, you noticed the strong smell of smoke. Even though people were allowed to smoke only at the bar, it still made your dinner experience unpleasant. Write an editorial in which you request that managers of the local restaurants make their establishments smoke-free. Clearly state your opinion on this issue and include two or three reasons to support your opinion. You may consider including the following reasons: respect for other customers of the restaurant, concern about the health of the servers, and the amount of time it takes for employees to clean up after smokers instead of serving more customers. Remember to develop your ideas fully and clearly and to write a strong conclusion summarizing your key points.

Prompts for Editorial Writing *(cont.)*

Prompt #7: Kindness to Animals

Quick Write: Brainstorm three reasons why it is important to be kind to animals.

Suppose you and your classmates want to start a "Kindness to Animals" campaign. Write an editorial for your school newspaper in which you request that all members of the school community be kind to animals, both pets and strays. Clearly state your opinion on this issue and include two or three reasons to support your opinion. To prepare for your editorial you may want to write a survey and find out how many of your classmates and teachers have pets. You may also want to call the Humane Society and find out how many strays have been found in your community recently. When your write your editorial, you may want to include the above statistics and include the following reasons for promoting kindness to animals: animals are innocent and deserve to be treated well, being kind to animals helps us practice our kindness to humans, and animals offer a great deal of comfort to humans and appreciate kindness in return. Remember to develop your ideas fully and clearly and to write a strong conclusion summarizing your key points.

Prompt #8: Eating a Balanced Diet

Quick Write: List three of your favorite foods.

Suppose you learn about eating a balanced diet in your science class. Write an editorial in which you promote the importance of eating a healthy diet. Clearly state your opinion on this issue and include two or three reasons to support your opinion. You may consider including the following reasons: eating a balanced diet gives you energy to complete your school assignments accurately, a good diet gives you the energy to play sports and do lots of extracurricular activities, and a good diet also allows you to maintain a healthy weight. Remember to develop your ideas fully and clearly and to write a strong conclusion summarizing your key points.

Prompts for Editorial Writing *(cont.)*

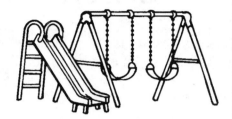

Prompt #9: Maintaining a Clean Community Playground

Quick Write: List three kinds of activities that you can do at a local playground.

Suppose you notice trash littering your community playground. Write an editorial for your school newspaper in which you request that members of the community do a better job cleaning up their trash once they decide to leave the playground. Clearly state your opinion on this issue and include two or three reasons to support your opinion. You may want to consider including the following reasons for requesting a clean community playground: respect for other members of the community, pride in your own community, and showing a good example to the younger members of the community. Remember to develop your ideas fully and clearly and to write a strong conclusion summarizing your key points.

Prompt #10: Discouraging Graffiti in School

Quick Write: List three of your favorite activities in school.

Suppose you and your classmates notice some graffiti on one of the school desks in your classroom. Write an editorial for your school newspaper in which you request that students refrain from writing graffiti on school property. Clearly state your opinion on this issue and include two or three reasons to support your opinion. You may consider including the following reasons: respect for other classmates in the school; respect for teachers; and promoting the reason for coming to school, which is to learn. Remember to develop your ideas fully and clearly and to write a strong conclusion summarizing your key points.

Criteria for Writing a Review

Objective: The student will identify the criteria for a review and use the criteria to examine sample reviews and write an original review.

Procedure

1. Write the definition of a review on the overhead or chalkboard: A *review* contains a summary or description of the subject being reviewed. A review also includes a critique of the subject being reviewed. The goal of the writer is to provide a balanced opinion of the subject.

2. Inform the students that an editorial has the following criteria:

   - a summary or description of the subject being reviewed

   - a balanced opinion of the subject being reviewed

   - support for the opinion

   - a strong conclusion that wraps up key points

3. Have students read the "Example of a Book Review" and identify the criteria in the sample review. Use the following questions to guide your discussion: Does the writer provide a good description or summary of the subject being reviewed? What is the writer's opinion of the subject? What support does the writer provide to back up his/her opinion? Is there a strong conclusion?

4. Use the prompts for review writing on pages 128–132 for student response.

5. Use the "Peer Response Form for a Review" on page 103 for the students to give each other feedback on their reviews.

6. Use the "Self" and "Peer" sections of the "Rubric for a Review" to allow the students an opportunity to evaluate their own reviews.

Portfolio Piece: Have students each write a reflection in which they identify the key points in the summary of their review. Have students reflect on whether or not they included all of the necessary information in their summaries.

Publishing: Have students create a TV talk show and share their reviews in front of the class as if they are professional movie or book reviewers.

Technology Connection: Have students use the Web to research background information for their reviews. Show students how to use a search engine to do a keyword search on a particular topic.

Home-School Connection: Instruct students to read a chapter from a book with a family member and summarize the key events from the chapter.

Assessment: Use the "Rubric for a Review" to evaluate the students' reviews.

Example of a Book Review

Directions: Read the following review carefully and think about the criteria for a review. Be prepared to discuss with your teacher the criteria for a review after you read.

Imagine a cold, snowy, Sunday afternoon in late January. The sky is milky and overcast, the snow falling at a rate of about an inch an hour. An icy winter wonderland is the setting at the opening of the young adult novel *Snow in the Afternoon*. In this book, Josephine Caruthers is the main character. She lives in Baltimore, Maryland, with her mom and stepdad. Josephine's mom is recently remarried and has not been paying a lot of attention to her in recent months. To make matters worse, Josephine's mom and stepdad are planning to move to Jacksonville, Florida, within the next two months. Josephine is saddened by her parents' decision, and she knows that she will miss the beautiful winter months in the town in which she was born.

The author, Jeanine Landon, does a good job of creating the character of Josephine. Landon describes Josephine as a tall 13-year-old girl with long brown hair and dark brown eyes. The author skillfully creates a picture of a wistful girl who loves her hometown and longs for her parents to get back together. Ms. Landon writes, "Josephine stared through her bedroom window at the crystal ice showers, longing for those days when she would shovel snow with her dad, knowing that a cup of hot chocolate was waiting for her when she came inside." Such imagery appeals to readers' senses and makes them want to keep reading.

Although some parts of the book are slow-moving, overall the author captures the feelings of loneliness that children experience when their parents get divorced and they have to move from their hometowns.

Example of a Movie Review

Directions: Read the following review carefully and think about the criteria for a review. Be prepared to discuss with your teacher the criteria for a review after you read.

How many times have you seen a movie in which the underdog somehow triumphs over those who appear to be stronger, braver, smarter, and more likely to succeed? *Football Frenzy* is a movie that fits the above description but still manages to be entertaining. Elbert is the name of the main character, but his friends call him Bert. Bert is small for his age, but he has the inner strength and determination of John Henry, the legendary hero of the railroad.

It has always been Bert's dream to play football, but none of the coaches will let him play because of his size and quiet demeanor. Bert gathers together some unlikely friends, and together they form their own football team. They spend several months training, practicing, eating healthy, and getting ready to prove to the coach that their team should be added to the league. The antics of Bert and his friends are humorous, and laughter keeps the movie moving at a fast pace.

Unfortunately, it is extremely easy for the viewer to predict what will happen next in *Football Frenzy.* The dialogue is a bit weak in spots; for example, the writers could have done a better job of coming up with original dialogue, especially between Bert and his coach. Despite the weak dialogue, and predictability of the plot, the non-stop humor and Bert's appealing character keep the audience engaged and interested.

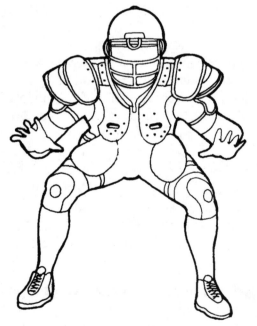

Overall, this is a movie to put on your list of weekend movies to rent. Make some popcorn, get cozy on the couch, and be entertained by a character who proves that we can all triumph no matter what obstacles we face. This is truly a movie that celebrates the human spirit.

Peer Response Form for a Review

Writer's name: _____ **Peer's name:**_____

Directions

- ❑ Read your draft aloud to your peer.
- ❑ Allow your peer to skim your review for the correct criteria.
- ❑ Ask your peer the following questions about your review.
- ❑ Take notes on what your peer says about how you can improve your draft. Remind your peer to give you specific examples from your draft.
- ❑ After you have completed this form, use a colored pencil to make necessary revisions based on your peer's comments.

1. How could my summary of the key events be more clear? _____

   _____

   _____

   _____

2. What is my opinion of the subject I am reviewing? _____

   _____

   _____

3. Do I provide a balanced opinion of the subject I am reviewing? How do you know?_____

   _____

   _____

   _____

4. What support do I provide for my opinion?

   a. _____

   _____

   b. _____

   _____

5. How could my conclusion be stronger? _____

   _____

   _____

Rubric for a Review

Writer: _____ Date: _____

Directions: Use the following rubric to evaluate your review.

	Self	Peer	Teacher
Completeness			
Content			
1. A summary or description adequately provides key information about the subject to the reader. (4)			
2. The writer's opinion of the subject is clearly stated. (2)			
3. The writer has provided adequate support for his/her opinion. (2)			
4. The conclusion summarizes the key idea(s) of the editorial. (2)			
Mechanics			
1. paragraphing (3)			
2. spelling (2)			
Total out of 15 points			

Writer's Reflection

1. What are your strengths in this review? _____

_____

_____

2. What do you plan to do to improve your review? _____

_____

_____

Finding the Subject for Review

Objective: The student will brainstorm a list of subjects for review, select one of those subjects, and determine the necessary action needed to prepare for the review.

Procedure

1. Revisit the definition of a review in the criteria lesson on page 100.

2. Pass out the reproducible entitled "Finding the Subject for Review." Lead a brainstorming session to help students complete the first question. Possible answers include books, stories, movies, plays, TV shows, music, entertainment parks, news magazines, articles, restaurants, etc.

3. Have students choose one of these subjects to review and help them pick something very specific to review. Examples: movie—*Star Wars*; book—*Little House on the Prairie* or *Anne of Green Gables*; story—*The Little Mermaid* or *Where the Wild Things Are*.

4. Discuss with the students the necessary actions needed to prepare for their review. Discuss with the students where they would need to go to read, listen, or view the choices related to the topics. Possible answers include the school or public library, the Internet, movie theatre, video store, record store, etc. Ask them to list on the reproducible the steps they would need to take.

5. Go to the library and allow the students to choose books and stories for review.

Portfolio Piece: Have students include their reviews in their portfolios. Instruct the students to reflect on their strengths and weaknesses in planning for their reviews.

Publishing: Create a bulletin board of the possible subjects and ideas for review and categorize the lists by books, movies, stories, songs, TV shows, etc.

Technology Connection: Have students use the Internet to research more subjects for review. Have them use the keyword search on such search engines as *Yahoo!*, *Infoseek*, or *Excite*. Check out the sites beforehand to make sure they are appropriate.

Home-School Connection: Have students brainstorm possible subjects for review with a family member. Remind the students to look in home libraries of magazines, books, and movies for ideas.

Assessment: Evaluate the students' abilities to complete the reproducible entitled "Finding the Subject for Review."

Finding the Subject for Review (cont.)

Directions: Complete the following worksheet in order to determine the subject for review.

1. Brainstorm five possible subjects for review. Circle the one on which you will focus. _____

   _____

   _____

   _____

   _____

   _____

2. Choose something very specific within the subject for review. _____

   _____

   _____

3. Brainstorm and prioritize a list of steps necessary to gather information on the subject.

Steps Necessary to Complete the Review	Priority

Standards and Benchmarks: 1A, 1D, 1J, 1K, 4A

Active Research

Objective: The student will use active research to gather information to write a review of a book or movie.

Procedure

1. Define active research for the students on the chalkboard or overhead: *Active research* involves reading, listening, and/or watching carefully to learn about the characters, setting, and conflict of a book, movie, or play. Often active research involves taking notes or filling out a graphic organizer while reading, viewing, and/or listening.

2. Read a short story to the students and have the students record the characters, settings, and conflict on the reproducible entitled "Active Research Guide." Remind the students to use the rating system to evaluate the author's development of characters, setting, and conflict.

3. After students have recorded the information, divide them into pairs and have them share their research guides with each other and make sure that they have the most complete responses. Encourage students to get ideas from each other to complete their worksheets.

4. Have the students use the information to write a review of the story.

5. Have students imagine they are reporters for the local newspaper and attend a movie, take notes on their research guides, and write a review of the movie.

6. Have students attend the school play and take notes on their research guides in order to write a review of the play.

Portfolio Piece: Instruct the students to include their active search notes in their portfolios. Have the students each write a reflection in which they identify their greatest challenge when taking notes on character, setting, and conflict in a story, movie, or play.

Publishing: Divide the students into pairs. Have one partner assume the persona of a radio talk show host and the other partner assume the persona of a professional reviewer. Have the talk-show host interview the reviewer about the story, movie, or play that was reviewed. Have the students share their performances with the class.

Technology Connection: Have the students research other reviews of the movies, stories, or plays they are reviewing. Have the students discuss how the reviewers gathered information on the characters, setting, or conflicts of the subjects they reviewed.

Home-School Connection: Instruct the students to watch a favorite TV show with a family member and take notes together on the "Active Research Guide."

Assessment: Evaluate the students' abilities to complete the "Active Research Guide" with detail and accuracy. Read the students' final reviews and evaluate their abilities to incorporate the information from their research into their reviews.

Active Research Guide

Directions: Use this guide when reading stories or books. You may also use this guide when watching/listening to movies or plays. Take careful notes because you will need to use these notes to write your review. In each category, circle your rating for the author's effectiveness.

Thumbs Up = Good	Thumbs Down = Needs Improvement

Title of book, story, movie, or play: _____

Characters

Identify main characters and briefly describe their personalities:

Thumbs Up   Thumbs Down

Setting

Describe the setting (both time and place):

Thumbs Up   Thumbs Down

Conflict

Describe the main conflict (problem):

Thumbs Up   Thumbs Down

Standards and Benchmarks: 1A, 1B, 1D, 1J, 1K, 4G

Identifying and Analyzing Conflict

Objective: The student will identify and analyze the conflict in a story with the purpose of writing a review of the story.

Procedure

1. Ask the students to define the word "conflict." Possible student responses include problems, difficulties, obstacles, hurdles, anger, fighting, and sadness. Inform the students that all high-quality stories have a meaningful conflict, an obstacle or obstacles that the main character has to overcome.

2. Instruct the students to read a short story. Then, have the students complete the worksheet entitled "Identifying and Analyzing Conflict." Encourage the students to revisit the text to answer the questions with adequate supporting details.

3. Have the students share their responses with a partner and make sure that their answers are complete and detailed.

4. Show the students how to use the information gained on their worksheets to summarize the main conflict of a story. Have the students highlight the most important information and then blend those ideas into a summary of the conflict. Then, guide the students to write the remaining components of the review of the story.

5. Have students watch a TV show, movie, or play and complete the "Identifying and Analyzing Conflict" worksheet.

Portfolio Piece: Have the students write a reflection in which they identify their greatest challenge when analyzing the conflict in a story.

Publishing: In round-robin fashion, have the students share their advice to their characters from their worksheets. On the chalkboard or overhead, record the students' responses. Then, as a class revise and shape the students' responses into a list poem.

Technology Connection: Go to the Amazon.com Web site and read three book reviews appropriate for students. Have the students examine the reviewers' abilities to identify and analyze conflicts.

Home-School Connection: Have the students discuss the following questions with a family member: "What obstacles do I face in my own life?" and "How do I overcome these obstacles?"

Assessment: Evaluate the students' "Identifying and Analyzing Conflict" worksheets for completeness and accuracy.

Identifying and Analyzing Conflict (cont.)

Directions: Use the following worksheet to identify and analyze conflict in a book, story, movie, play, or TV show.

1. What is the first event that causes the main character difficulty? _____

   _____

   _____

   _____

2. What is the character's reaction to this difficulty? _____

   _____

   _____

   _____

3. Does the character's reaction cause a new problem to arise? Explain. _____

   _____

   _____

   _____

4. What is the main conflict or problem carried throughout the plot? Explain in detail. _____

   _____

   _____

   _____

   _____

5. How does the author use conflicts or problems to draw the reader into the plot? _____

   _____

   _____

   _____

6. What two pieces of advice would you give to the main character to help him or her solve the main conflict? _____

   _____

   _____

   _____

   _____

Audience in Review Writing

Objective: The student will use knowledge of the audience to write a balanced and informative review of a book, movie, or play.

Procedure

1. Read a favorite children's story to the students. After you are finished reading, ask the students what the author knew about what children like in a story. Have them refer to specific parts of the text to support their answers. Inform the students that writers need to be knowledgeable about their audience before they begin to write.

2. Read aloud the questions on the reproducible entitled "Audience-Analysis Guide for Reviews" and read aloud the "Example of a Movie Review" on page 102. Pause during your reading to discuss the clues the author gives about knowledge of the audience.

3. Have students complete the "Audience-Analysis Guide for Reviews" in response to the movie review. Encourage students to answer all of the questions and make inferences, if necessary. Remind the students to draw on their own lives and personal experiences since they are part of the intended audience.

4. Ask the students to find specific places in the text of the review that show that the author is using his/her knowledge of the audience.

5. Read a favorite poem to the students and discuss the author's knowledge of the audience. Ask the students, "Does the author understand his/her audience? How do you know?"

Portfolio Piece: After students have written reviews, have them highlight sentences where they used what they knew about the audience. Have the students each choose their best sentence and write an explanation of how this sentence will appeal to the audience.

Publishing: Divide the students into pairs and have them read their reviews aloud to each other. As each writer reads his/her review, have the listeners record words or phrases that show knowledge of the audience.

Technology Connection: Have students read reviews online and complete the analysis guide. Ask the question, "What assumptions do online authors make about the audience that are different from those made by authors of articles, stories, and poems that are not online?" (Example: Online authors assume that the audience will click on colored links within the text.)

Home-School Connection: Have the students each find an ad in a magazine and discuss with a family member the assumptions the creator(s) makes about the audience.

Assessment: Evaluate the students' thoughtful completions of the reproducible entitled "Audience-Analysis Guide for Reviews."

Audience-Analysis Guide for Reviews

Directions: Competent writers always have a "picture" in their minds of their intended audiences. If you think about the audience before you write, you will be better able to write a review that meets the audience's needs. Respond to the following questions in order to get to know the audience.

Remember: The audience for your review may not have actually experienced what you are reviewing.

Tip: There may be multiple answers for each question.

1. What is the age group and gender of the intended audience? _____
   _____
   _____

2. What is the highest level of education of the audience? _____
   _____
   _____

3. What does the audience already know about the book, movie, or play?_____
   _____
   _____

4. What background information does the audience need to know in order to understand the story in the book, movie, or play? _____
   _____
   _____

5. What does the audience appreciate in a good book, movie, or play? _____
   _____

6. Does the audience respect the reviewer? _____
   _____
   _____

7. What topics does the audience care about in a book, movie, or play? _____
   _____

8. What elements of a book, movie, or play make the audience cry? _____
   _____

9. What elements of a book, movie, or play make the audience laugh? _____
   _____
   _____

10. What are the audience's expectations for the conclusion of a book, movie, or play? _____
    _____
    _____

Making Generalizations

Objective: The student will write a generalization derived from research information and support the generalization with specific examples from the subject being reviewed.

Procedure

1. Define the word *generalization* for the students: A generalization is a broad statement that can be applied to a variety of situations. When making generalizations, readers/viewers notice similarities among the subjects they are observing. Often it necessary to rely on your personal experience and prior knowledge to make a generalization.

2. Pass out three movie reviews from the local newspaper. Have the students take notes about the reviews on their worksheets entitled "Making Generalizations."

3. Divide the students into pairs and have them make sure that their notes are complete. As a class, review the notes and model for the students how to determine the important details to write on the reproducible.

4. As a class, determine the similarities among the movie reviews. Guide the students to make simple observations, such as: "All of the reviews mentioned the main characters' names" or "All of the reviews commented on the plot or conflict."

5. Have each student individually write a generalization about movie reviews by rereading the similarities and either choosing one or blending the observations together. For example: "Movie reviews mention some of the characters and refer to the major plot line." Share generalizations and help the students revise their statements to make them clear and succinct.

6. Read newspaper and magazine articles and identify the authors' generalizations.

Portfolio Piece: Have students each write a reflection about their review and identify any generalizations that they made. Have students reflect on how they used their personal experiences to make general observations about the characters, settings, or conflicts.

Publishing: Have students share their generalizations in a round-robin fashion. Be sure to offer praise and comment on the students' growth in making generalizations.

Technology Connection: Have students use a word-processing program for the revision process. Students will need to add and delete to tighten their generalizations.

Home-School Connection: Have students each read two children's stories with a family member and make one generalization about children's stories.

Assessment: Evaluate students' completions of the reproducible entitled "Making Generalizations." Evaluate the students' abilities to use generalizations appropriately in their review writing.

Making Generalizations (cont.)

Directions: Read three movie reviews from the local newspaper and take notes in the spaces provided. Next, identify two similarities among the reviews. Finally, make a generalization about movie reviews.

Remember: A generalization is a broad statement that can be applied to a variety of situations. When making generalizations, readers/viewers notice similarities among the subjects they are observing.

Movie Review #1 Notes

Movie Review #2 Notes

Movie Review #3 Notes

Similarities among the reviews: _____

_____

_____

_____

Generalization about movie reviews: _____

_____

_____

_____

Supporting and Balancing Your Opinion

Objective: The student will write about the strengths and weaknesses of a school play or a movie in order to present a balanced opinion to the reader.

Procedure

1. Read aloud the sample movie review on page 102.

2. Write an opinion statement about the review. Model for the class how to write this statement, using the following sentence starter: Overall, I liked/disliked the author's approach to the subject because. . . .

3. Have the students watch the school play or a movie relevant to your curriculum. Instruct the students to use the reproducible entitled "Using Details and Descriptions" on page 118 to take notes while they are viewing.

4. Instruct the students to use their notes to complete the reproducible entitled "Supporting and Balancing Your Opinion." Guide the students when identifying the strengths and weaknesses of the movie or play.

5. Have the students use the reproducible to write balanced reviews. Remind them to each write a controlled opinion statement and to use transitions to link their ideas.

6. Read reviews in the newspaper and use the reproducible to record strengths and weaknesses of the subject identified in the review. Discuss whether or not the author presented a balanced opinion.

7. Give students photographs to look at. Ask them to evaluate the strengths and weaknesses of the photographs based on the following criteria: the lighting, the positioning of the subject in the photograph, and the clarity of the picture.

Portfolio Piece: Have the students include their balanced reviews in their portfolios. Instruct them to reflect upon whether or not they provided adequate and balanced supports for their overall opinions.

Publishing: Have students share their opinions and encourage the students to critique each other on their selections of specific examples from the movie or play to support their opinions. Create a bulletin board of reviews with balanced opinions.

Technology Connection: Partner the students in the school's computer lab and instruct them to read each other's drafts out loud and make recommendations about what to add, delete, or change in order to balance the reviews.

Home-School Connection: Instruct students to review a favorite family restaurant. Have them each use the reproducible to record the strengths and weaknesses of the restaurant.

Assessment: Evaluate the students' abilities to write balanced reviews. Students should identify at least two strengths and weaknesses about their subjects on the reproducible entitled "Supporting and Balancing Your Opinion."

Supporting and Balancing Your Opinion *(cont.)*

Directions: Complete the following chart and use specific examples from the story, book, song, play, movie, TV show, etc.

Remember: It is important to present a balanced opinion so that the reader will take you seriously.

Author's Overall Opinion of the Subject: _____

Strengths (What worked?)	Weaknesses (What didn't work?)

Concluding Ideas:_____

_____

_____

_____

Using Details and Descriptions

Objective: The student will use details and descriptions about titles, characters, setting, and conflict so that the review makes sense to the reader.

Procedure

1. Share with the students the following sentence: "The girl ran down the stairs." Tell the students that the sentence is a detailed summary of a classic story. Students should respond by identifying that the sentence is not a detailed summary of the story. Have the students ask questions about the words in the sentence in order to clarify and expand the sentence. As students ask questions, reveal to them that the girl is Cinderella and that she ran down the stairs at the stroke of midnight in order to escape from the prince. Inform the students that authors must always support their main ideas with details and descriptions in order for readers to understand what happened in the story.

2. Share with the students the reproducible "Using Details and Descriptions." Instruct them to read a book or a story and keep the categories of the reproducible in mind as they read. Encourage them to take notes as they read.

3. After the students have read, tell them that their purpose is to inform their audience about the essential elements of plot and to critique the book or story so that the members of the audience know whether or not to read it themselves.

4. Have students write their reviews using their notes from the reproducible. Remind the students to use transitions between ideas and to make sure that their language is unemotional. Clear, unemotional language convinces the reader that the reviewer is logical and his/her opinions are to be trusted.

5. Divide the students into groups of two. Have each group member read the same story and complete the reproducible. Then have them compare notes and make sure that they have gathered all of the necessary details in order to write a balanced review.

Portfolio Piece: Have students each write a reflection about the importance of details and descriptions. Have them each identify a place in their reviews that could use description, add the necessary information, and then identify why their review is better.

Publishing: Create a class anthology of book reviews and have the anthology displayed in the library for other students to use as a resource when selecting books.

Technology Connection: Have students post their reviews on the school's Web site. Instruct students to use a word-processing program to add and delete details and descriptions as appropriate to their audience and purpose.

Home-School Connection: Instruct students to watch an appropriate TV show with a family member and complete the "Using Details and Descriptions" reproducible.

Assessment: Use the rubric on page 104 to evaluate the students' reviews for adequate details and descriptions.

Using Details and Descriptions *(cont.)*

Directions: Use this worksheet to identify the details and descriptions you will use for your review of a book, movie, or play.

Part I

Character	Physical Description	Character Traits

Part II

Major Setting	Adjectives and Sensory Details to Describe the Setting

Part III

Details about the problem (summarize) _____

_____

_____

_____

Using Vivid Verbs

Objective: The student will use vivid verbs in review writing to enhance the meaning of the text.

Procedure

1. Have the students brainstorm some action verbs. Sample responses include *run, jump, hide, swim, talk,* and *climb.* Ask the students to define the word *verb.* Students should respond that verbs show action.

2. Pass out the reproducible entitled "Using Vivid Verbs." Review with the students the complete definition of verbs. Have the students complete Parts A and B of the "Writer's Practice" section.

3. Have the students take out the drafts of their reviews and highlight all of the verbs. Instruct the students to replace ordinary verbs with vivid verbs that specifically express their intent as writers.

4. Instruct the students to switch papers with a peer and brainstorm vivid verbs that could replace ordinary verbs in their drafts.

5. Brainstorm 35–40 vivid verbs and write each of them on an index card. Pass out a word list for the students to use as a reference. Then distribute one card to each student and have students act out their verbs one by one in front of the class. Students in the audience guess the words by looking at their word list and watching the student performance carefully.

Portfolio Piece: Have the students reflect on the importance of using vivid verbs. In their reflections, have the students list three ways that they can improve their use of verbs. Students should respond that they could reread, highlight, and replace; get a peer to help; refer to the word bank; use a dictionary or thesaurus; or ask the teacher for assistance.

Publishing: Create a vivid-verb wall. Give each student five "red bricks" cut out of red construction paper and ask the students to write a vivid verb on one brick every night for a week. At the end of the week, have the students bring in their "bricks" and assemble the verb wall in an appropriate part of the classroom.

Technology Connection: Have the students use the thesaurus function in a word-processing program to look up additional synonyms for ordinary verbs.

Home-School Connection: Instruct the students to each read a newspaper article or review with a family member and change three ordinary verbs to vivid verbs.

Assessment: Evaluate the students' understanding of vivid verbs by checking the "Using Vivid Verbs" reproducible for completeness and accuracy. Read the students' reviews and determine whether they have applied their knowledge of vivid verbs to their writing.

Using Vivid Verbs *(cont.)*

Directions: Read the information below and then complete the "Writer's Practice" section below.

> A **verb** is a word that shows action or expresses a state of being. A sentence must have a verb in order to be complete.
>
> An **action verb** shows action by telling what someone or something does. The action can be physical (such as jumping, running, climbing) or emotional/mental (such as reflecting, pondering, wondering, loving).

Writer's Practice

Part A: Complete the following sentences with vivid action verbs.

1. The girl _____ to the store on the windy afternoon.

2. The thunder _____ in the sky as the trees swayed in the wind.

3. The deer_____ through the field to escape the predator.

4. The boy _____ when he found out that he won the spelling bee.

5. The frog_____ across the stream to reach the other side.

Part B: Brainstorm four vivid action verbs for each of the following ordinary action verbs listed below.

Ordinary Verbs	Vivid Verbs
run	
walk	
said	
like	
think	

Mood

Objective: The student will write a paragraph in which he/she identifies how the subject of a story or song influenced his/her feelings and thoughts.

Procedure

1. Show the students a series of drawn faces that each have a different expression that reveals an emotion. As you show them the faces, discuss with them the expressions. Use the following question to guide your discussion: "Does this person feel sad, happy, outraged, supportive, excited, or amazed?"

2. Inform the students that mood is the feeling that the audience has after reading the work of a particular author, listening to a song, or watching a movie.

3. Have students read a story or listen to a song. (Choose a song that has a narrative.) When you have finished reading the story or listening to the song, lead a discussion about how the subject influenced the students' feelings and thoughts. Use the following question to guide your discussion: "Did you feel [sad, happy, outraged, supportive, excited, amazed, scared, or another emotion] as a result of reading the story or listening to the song?" Have students choose specific words, phrases, or sentences from the story or song that helped to influence their feelings. Use the reproducible entitled "Identifying Mood" to guide your discussion.

4. Divide the students into pairs and have them read aloud the rough drafts of their reviews and identify the mood (if any) that they feel as a result of listening to their partner's drafts.

5. Instruct students to each write a paragraph about the story they read or the song to which they listened. After writing, students should highlight words or phrases that reveal their feelings and thoughts about the subject.

6. Divide students into pairs and have them read each other's paragraphs. Instruct partners to identify specific words and phrases in the paragraph that reveal the writer's feelings and thoughts about the subject.

Portfolio Piece: Have students include their paragraphs in their portfolios and each write a reflection on the importance of connecting with the thoughts and feelings of the audience.

Publishing: Have students write original survival stories. Then have them share their survival stories in groups of four or five and identify the moods of the listeners as the authors share their stories. (Possible feelings: fear, concern, anxiety, frustration, etc.)

Technology Connection: Create a bulletin board of reviews and categorize the reviews according to the feelings of the writers about the subjects being reviewed.

Home-School Connection: Have students look through magazines with a family member and focus on their moods when viewing the advertisements.

Assessment: Use the rubric on page 104 to score the student's book/song review.

Identifying Mood

Directions: Use this worksheet to identify how the subject influences you as a reader, listener, or viewer.

Title: _____

Circle one: **book**   **story**   **song**   **movie**   **TV show**   **play**

Elements of a Story (Character, Setting, Plot)	Your Resulting Feelings and Thoughts
Words, phrases, or sentences spoken by or about a character:	
Words, phrases, or sentences about the setting:	
Words, phrases, or sentences that reveal the plot:	

Do you think your mood as a result of reading/listening/watching was what the author intended you to feel? Why or why not? _____

_____

_____

Standards and Benchmarks: 1A, 1B, 1D, 1J, 1K, 3E

Tense

Objective: The student will write a review and use the present tense.

Procedure

1. Share with the students the following information about verbs: Verbs reveal time. The *tense* of a verb reveals the time that the verb is trying to show the audience.

2. Have students brainstorm verbs. As the students share ideas, categorize their verbs on the chalkboard into a chart that has the following categories: past tense, present tense, and future tense.

3. Have the students complete the "Writer's Practice" section on the reproducible entitled "Verb Tense."

4. Instruct students to write their own reviews in the present tense.

5. During the revision process, instruct the students to go through their reviews and highlight their verbs. Have them change any verbs that are not in present tense.

6. Divide the students into pairs. Have them switch papers and take turns checking their drafts for verbs written in the present tense.

7. Instruct students to correct any verbs in their rough drafts by writing the present tense of the verb on their drafts in colored pencil to make writing the publishable draft easier.

8. Have students create a word list of the most common present tense verbs that authors use when writing reviews.

Portfolio Piece: Have students highlight their present-tense verbs and write a reflection in which they identify the greatest challenge that they faced when keeping their verbs in the present tense.

Publishing: Create a bulletin board of most commonly used present tense verbs for the students to use as a reference.

Technology Connection: Have students use the grammar checking function to make sure that they have subject-verb agreement throughout their reviews.

Home-School Connection: Instruct students to read a children's book with a family member, identify all the verbs, and categorize the verbs according to past, present, and future tenses.

Assessment: Use the rubric on page 104 to score the students' reviews. Read the review carefully for verbs written in the present tense. Require the students to go back and revise if they have not used present-tense verbs correctly.

Verb Tense

Directions: Read the information below about the present, past, and future tenses of verbs. Then complete the "Writer's Practice" section below.

Remember: The tense of a verb reveals time.

Verbs in the **present tense** show action that is happening now.
Example: We *run* through the streets.

Verbs in the **past tense** show action that has already happened.
Example: We *ran* through the streets.

Verbs in the **future tense** show action that is going to happen in the future.
Example: We *will be running* through the streets.

Writer's Practice

Use each of the present tense verbs below in original sentences.

1. see _____

_____

2. learn _____

_____

3. watch _____

_____

4. jump _____

_____

5. wonder _____

_____

6. play _____

_____

7. sing _____

_____

8. dig _____

_____

9. walk _____

_____

10. talk _____

_____

Punctuating Titles

Objective: The student will correctly punctuate the titles of stories, poems, plays, articles, movies, TV shows, and books in review writing.

Procedure

1. Read aloud to the students the rule for punctuating titles included at the top of the reproducible entitled "Punctuating Titles."

2. Have the students complete the "Writer's Practice" section on the reproducible.

3. Instruct the students to reread the drafts of their reviews and identify any titles that they have included in the texts of their reviews. Have the students reread the rule and correctly punctuate any titles in their reviews.

4. Divide the students into pairs and have them read each other's drafts and make sure that they have punctuated titles correctly.

5. Have the students read reviews of books and movies from the newspaper. Have them highlight all of the titles and make sure they are correctly punctuated.

Portfolio Piece: Have the students include their reviews in their portfolios and each write a reflection about the importance of correctly punctuating titles. Students should identify that readers expect writers to use rules and conventions. When writers follow the rules, then the reader will be more likely to respect the writer's opinion in the review.

Publishing: Photocopy and collate the students' reviews into a class set. Save one book of student reviews that have correctly punctuated titles in order to serve as examples for other classes.

Technology Connection: Use a word-processing program to type the reviews. Use the italics function to punctuate book titles and use quotation marks to punctuate shorter works such as stories, poems, and TV shows.

Home-School Connection: Instruct students to read reviews of books or movies at home with a family member and check to see that the author has punctuated the titles correctly.

Assessment: Evaluate the students' abilities to punctuate titles correctly by checking the "Writer's Practice" of the reproducible for completeness and accuracy. Also, read the students' drafts of their reviews to make sure that the students have applied their knowledge of punctuating titles to their writing.

Punctuating Titles *(cont.)*

Directions: Read the following rule about punctuating titles. Then, complete the exercises in the "Writer's Practice" section.

> **Rule:** When punctuating titles, italicize or underline the titles of books, professional journals, TV shows, movies, and magazines. For shorter works such as articles, short stories, and poems, punctuate the titles with quotation marks.

Writer's Practice

Punctuate the following titles correctly within the sentence.

1. I really enjoyed reading the book Hatchet by Gary Paulsen.

2. One of the best poems I have ever read is If by Rudyard Kipling.

3. The TV show Seventh Heaven has very likeable characters.

4. I read an article entitled Dogs are Man's Best Friend in a magazine recently.

5. We went to see the play The Glass Menagerie by Tennessee Williams.

6. The book 10,000 Leagues Under the Sea by Jules Verne is extremely adventurous.

7. In the movie October Sky, the main characters create a rocket that wins the top award at a national science fair.

8. This weekend we went to Broadway to see the play The Lion King.

9. Robert Frost wrote the poem The Road Not Taken.

10. In The Indian in the Cupboard series, Lynn Reid Banks stimulates the readers' imaginations.

Standards and Benchmarks: 1A, 1B, 1C, 1D, 1E, 1G

Responding to Prompts for Review Writing

Objective: The student will respond to a prompt for review writing by stating an opinion of the subject being reviewed, supporting the opinions with detailed examples, and balancing the opinions in order to meet the needs of the intended audience.

Procedure

1. Use the previous lessons in the review writing section to teach the students how to develop and organize their reviews as well as support and balance their opinions with detailed examples. Show students the "Rubric for a Review" on page 104 in order to demonstrate how their reviews will be evaluated.

2. Pass out one of the prompts for review writing (pages 128–132) and instruct the students to respond to the corresponding "Quick Write." Students should respond to this question as quickly as possible because it is intended to prod the students' thinking. Tip: Vary the amount that the students have to write according to ability level.

3. Instruct the students to respond to the prompt. Guide and encourage the students as they are drafting their responses.

4. Have students use the "Peer Response Form for a Review" on page 103 to give each other feedback. Instruct the students to revise and redraft as necessary in order to produce a publishable draft.

5. Divide the students into pairs and have them engage in a role-playing scenario in which one student is the author of the review and the other student is the audience for the review. Have the student who is portraying the "audience" ask the writer for clarification on different points in the review.

Portfolio Piece: Have students respond to many of the prompts and each choose their favorite response for inclusion in their portfolios. Have them each write a reflection in which they justify their choices with examples from the text of their reviews.

Publishing: Instruct the students to submit their reviews directly to the editor of the school magazine or newspaper.

Technology Connection: Have students scan photographs of the subject being reviewed into the text of their review.

Home-School Connection: Instruct students to each write an original prompt with a family member, bring the prompt to class, and share with classmates.

Assessment: Use the "Rubric for a Review" on page 104 to evaluate the students' responses to the prompts.

Prompts for Review Writing

Prompt #1: Reviewing a Story

Quick Write: Who are the main characters and what is the setting of the story you just read?

Suppose your teacher has asked you to write a review of a story you just read in class. Summarize for your teacher the characters, setting, and problem in the story that you read. Next, state your opinion of the story. Support your opinion with specific examples from the text. Remember to provide a balanced opinion. If your opinion of the story is mostly negative, try to mention some things that you liked. If your opinion of the story is mostly positive, try to mention some things that could be improved. Write a conclusion that summarizes your key points. Remember to write clearly and concisely and to provide adequate support from the text for all of your ideas.

Prompt #2: Reviewing a Movie

Quick Write: Who are the main characters, and what is the setting of a movie you have seen recently?

Suppose your teacher has asked you to write a review of a movie you have seen recently. Summarize for your teacher the characters, setting, and problem in the movie that you watched. Next, state your opinion of the movie and support your opinion with specific examples from the movie (refer to the beginning of the movie, the end of the movie, the development of the characters, the dialogue of the characters, the choice of setting, and the problem). Are the characters like real-life people? Does the beginning of the movie grab the viewer? Is the problem one that the audience will care about? Remember to provide a balanced opinion. If your opinion of the movie is mostly negative, try to mention some things that you liked. If your opinion of the movie is mostly positive, try to mention some things that could be improved. Write a conclusion that summarizes your key points. Remember to write clearly and concisely and to provide adequate support from the movie for all of your ideas.

Prompts for Review Writing *(cont.)*

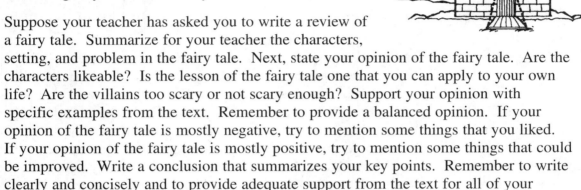

Prompt #3: Reviewing a Fairy Tale

Quick Write: Who are the main characters, and what is the setting of your favorite fairy tale?

Suppose your teacher has asked you to write a review of a fairy tale. Summarize for your teacher the characters, setting, and problem in the fairy tale. Next, state your opinion of the fairy tale. Are the characters likeable? Is the lesson of the fairy tale one that you can apply to your own life? Are the villains too scary or not scary enough? Support your opinion with specific examples from the text. Remember to provide a balanced opinion. If your opinion of the fairy tale is mostly negative, try to mention some things that you liked. If your opinion of the fairy tale is mostly positive, try to mention some things that could be improved. Write a conclusion that summarizes your key points. Remember to write clearly and concisely and to provide adequate support from the text for all of your ideas.

Prompt #4: Reviewing a Children's Book

Quick Write: List three of your favorite children's books.

Suppose your teacher has asked you to write a review of a children's book. Summarize for your teacher the characters, setting, and problem of the children's book. Next, state your opinion of the book and support your opinion with specific examples from the book. Remember to refer to the beginning and end of the book, the development of the characters, the dialogue of the characters, the choice of setting, and the problem. Do the illustrations complement the story? Does the author use rhythm and rhyme appropriately? Is the problem one that the audience will care about? Remember to provide a balanced opinion. If your opinion of the book is mostly negative, try to mention some things that you liked. If your opinion of the book is mostly positive, try to mention some things that could be improved. Write a conclusion that summarizes your key points. Remember to write clearly and concisely and to provide adequate support from the book for all of your ideas.

Prompts for Review Writing (cont.)

Prompt #5: Reviewing a Cereal

Quick Write: List three of your favorite breakfast cereals.

Suppose your teacher has asked you to write a review of a breakfast cereal. Summarize for your teacher the taste, nutritional value, and price of the cereal. You may also want to comment on the packaging of the cereal, including the advertiser's use of color, design, characters, and recipes to attract your attention. Next, state your opinion of the cereal. Support your opinion with specific examples about the cereal. Remember to provide a balanced opinion. If your opinion of the cereal is mostly negative, try to mention some things that you liked. If your opinion of the cereal is mostly positive, try to mention some things that could be improved. Write a conclusion that summarizes your key points. Remember to write clearly and concisely and to provide adequate support with details about the cereal for all of your ideas.

Prompt #6: Reviewing a Kid's Magazine

Quick Write: List two of your favorite kids magazines.

Suppose your teacher has asked you to write a review of a kids' magazine. Summarize for your teacher the topics, games, activities, and main focus of the magazine. You may also want to comment on the illustrations, photographs, and advertisements included in the magazine. Next, state your opinion of the magazine and support your opinion with specific examples. Are the features interesting? Are the games and activities fun to play? Remember to provide a balanced opinion. If your opinion of the magazine is mostly negative, try to mention some things that you liked. If your opinion of the magazine is mostly positive, try to mention some things that could be improved. Write a conclusion that summarizes your key points. Remember to write clearly and concisely and to provide adequate support from the magazine for all of your ideas.

Prompts for Review Writing *(cont.)*

Prompt #7: Reviewing a Board Game

Quick Write: List three of your favorite board games.

Suppose your teacher has asked you to write a review of a board game. Summarize for your teacher the rules, the game pieces, and the objective the game. You may also want to comment on the design of the game board and any game pieces that are particularly clever or attractive. Next, state your opinion of the board game. Support your opinion with specific examples from the game. Remember to provide a balanced opinion. If your opinion of the game is mostly negative, try to mention some things that you liked. If your opinion of the game is mostly positive, try to mention some things that could be improved. Write a conclusion that summarizes your key points. Remember to write clearly and concisely and to provide adequate support from the game for all of your ideas.

Prompt #8: Reviewing a Play

Quick Write: Who are the main characters, and what is the setting of a play you have seen recently?

Suppose your teacher has asked you to write a review of a play you have seen recently. Summarize for your teacher the characters, setting, and problem of the play you watched. Next, state your opinion of the play and support your opinion with specific examples from the play. Refer to the beginning and end of the play, the development of the characters, the dialogue of the characters, the choice of setting, and the problem. Are the characters like real-life people? Does the beginning of the play grab the viewer? Is the problem one that the audience will care about? Remember to provide a balanced opinion. If your opinion of the play is mostly negative, try to mention some things that you liked. If your opinion of the play is mostly positive, try to mention some things that could be improved. Write a conclusion that summarizes your key points. Remember to write clearly and concisely and to provide adequate support from the play for all of your ideas.

Prompts for Review Writing *(cont.)*

Prompt #9: Reviewing a Musical Performance

Quick Write: List three of your favorite songs. Identify any similarities among the songs.

Suppose your teacher has asked you to write a review of a musical performance. Summarize for your teacher the themes, tempos, and lyrics of a few of the songs in the performance. Comment on the feelings or emotions that the music was intended to evoke in the audience. Next, state your opinion of the musical performance. Support your opinion with specific examples from the performance. Remember to provide a balanced opinion. If your opinion of the performance is mostly negative, try to mention some things that you liked. If your opinion of the performance is mostly positive, try to mention some things that could be improved. Write a conclusion that summarizes your key points. Remember to write clearly and concisely and to provide adequate support from the musical performance for all of your ideas.

Prompt #10: Reviewing an Educational Software Program

Quick Write: What are some of your favorite educational software programs?

Suppose your teacher has asked you to write a review of an educational software program. Summarize for your teacher the learning objective, characters, and rules of the software program. You may also consider describing the graphics and sound effects included in the program. Next, state your opinion of the program and support your opinion by using specific examples. Is the content that you are supposed to learn meaningful? Is the program fun and engaging? Remember to provide a balanced opinion. If your opinion of the software program is mostly negative, try to mention some things that you liked. If your opinion of the software program is mostly positive, try to mention some things that could be improved. Write a conclusion that summarizes your key points. Remember to write clearly and concisely and to provide adequate support from the program for all of your ideas.

Standards and Benchmarks: 1A, 1B, 1C, 1D, 1E, 1F, 1G, 1J, 2A, 2B, 3K, 3L, 4A, 4B, 4F, 4G

Final Assessment

Say No! to Smoking

Objectives: The student will write a letter to the editor of the newspaper informing children and adults of the negative effects of smoking. The student will use precise language to inform the audience, make clear generalizations and support them with evidence and specific details.

Procedure

1. Begin by reading aloud the Introduction on page 135. Review the checklist that outlines the required activities for the students.

2. Have the students read the "Smoking Facts Sheet" and highlight key ideas in each of the fact statements. Guide the students while they are identifying key ideas.

3. Instruct the students to make three generalizations about the harmful effects of smoking. Next, take the students to the library and have them use resources to gather information to support their generalizations. Guide the students to use the following resources: books, magazines, newspapers, pamphlets, brochures, encyclopedias, and online sources.

4. Circulate around the room and offer guidance as the students complete the graphic organizer on page 138.

5. Instruct the students to read the "Prewriting Guidelines" on page 139 and write their rough drafts, using their graphic organizers to guide them.

6. Have the students complete the self-revision activity on page 140. Provide the students with colored pencils for circling and underlining the necessary parts of their rough drafts.

7. Divide the students into pairs and have them complete the peer response activity on page 141. Remind the students to offer their suggestions and to answer the questions in a polite manner.

8. Have the students complete the proofreading activity. Suggest to the students that they reread their drafts and answer each question one at a time. This is a time-consuming process and requires much patience from the students. Model for the students how to read carefully for engaging leads, effective transitions, elements of style, effective word choice, varied sentence structure and length.

9. Have the students use their self-revision, peer response, and proofreading activities to write their publishable drafts of their letters to the editor of the local newspaper about the seriously harmful effects of cigarette smoking.

Say No! to Smoking *(cont.)*

Portfolio Piece: Have the students include a copy of their letters to the editor in their portfolios. In addition, have the students complete the "Audience-Analysis Guide for Editorial Writing" on page 65 before they write their letters. After the letters are written, have the students identify three strengths in appealing to the audience.

Publishing: (1) Have students mail their letters to the editor of the local newspaper. (2) Organize a school assembly, and have the students read their letters to the audience and discuss ways that members of the community can increase the awareness of the harmful effects of smoking. (3) Write a letter to area restaurants requesting that the manager make his/her establishment smoke-free. In your letter, be sure to state that you are against smoking and give at least three reasons to support your position. Back up your reasons with examples and statistics from text, personal experience, and class activities. (4) Write a letter to local government officials informing them that you want them to encourage restaurants to be smoke-free and to remind local gas stations and convenience stores not to sell cigarettes to those who are underage. (5) Write a letter to the local police department asking officers to discourage kids who smoke and loiter outside of malls and fast-food restaurants. (6) Make sure that students use the conventions of capitalization and punctuation in their publishable drafts.

Technology Connection: (1) Have students create a multi-media slideshow in which they demonstrate the negative effects of smoking with facts and photographs from the American Heart Association, the American Cancer Society, and the Center for Disease Control. (2) Write a smoke-free school mission and post it on the school Web site. At the site, create links to the Surgeon General's Web Site for Kids, the American Heart Association, and other sites associated with informing the public about the negative effects of smoking. (3) Have the students use a search engine to do a keyword search on cigarette smoking. Instruct the students to make a list of useful Web sites that could serve as resources to teachers, parents, and other students in the community. (4) Have students use a word-processing program to type their final letters to the editor. Instruct the students to use appropriate fonts and graphics to enhance their texts. Also, instruct the students to draft, revise, and edit their letters to the editor in order to produce publishable drafts.

Home-School Connection: Sponsor a "Family Night" at your school. At this event, have students inform community members of the negative effects of smoking. Have the students present other sources of information. Then, have families play board games. Serve snacks and other light refreshments.

Assessment: Use the "Final Assessment Rubric" on page 144 to assess the students' letters to the editor. Allow the students an opportunity to complete the "Self" column and assess their own abilities to fulfill the requirements of the assignment. Also, provide the students with an opportunity to complete the "Peer" column on the rubric. Divide the students into pairs and have them give each other feedback on the five components of the letter to the editor identified on the rubric. Discuss with the students any responses that they receive as a result of their letters.

Cross-Curricular Connections: In social studies classes, have the students examine smoking advertisements and identify the ways that cigarette companies shape our opinions of smoking. In science classes, inform the students about the effects of smoking on the body. Use pictures of the human body to target specific areas that are affected. In math classes, have the students make bar graphs and circle graphs after reading statistics related to smoking trends in the region, state, and nation.

Final Assessment *(cont.)*

Introduction

It is a known fact that smoking is very harmful to our health. Smoking can seriously harm our hearts, lungs, throats, and mouths. Despite these severe consequences, many people—including young kids—continue to smoke. Write a letter to the editor of your local newspaper in which you inform children and adults about the negative effects of smoking. Complete the following activities to prepare for writing a polished, publishable draft.

❑ Read the "Smoking Facts Sheet." (page 136)

❑ Use the "Research Guide" (page 137) to make three generalizations about the harmful effects of smoking and research these generalizations by using resources in the school library.

❑ Complete the "Persuasive Writing Graphic Organizer." (page 138)

❑ Read the "Prewriting Guidelines." (page 139)

❑ Read the "Final Prompt." (page 143)

❑ Write a rough draft.

❑ Complete the "Self-Revision Activity." (page 140)

❑ Complete the "Peer Response Activity." (page 141)

❑ Complete the "Proofreading Questions." (page 142)

❑ Write the final draft.

❑ Use the "Final Assessment Rubric" (page 144) to evaluate the final letter.

Final Assessment *(cont.)*

Smoking Facts Sheet

Directions: Read the following facts. As you read, highlight the key idea in each of the fact statements.

Children who start smoking are more likely to get lower grades in school. These kids usually spend time with other kids who smoke. These kids may have low self-images, and they may not know how to refuse tobacco.

Cigarette advertisers want to make people think that smoking is cool and that everybody is doing it. Misleading cigarette ads seem to increase kids' risk of smoking.

Good news! Kids who warn each other about the dangers of smoking seem to be able to keep some kids away from smoking.

Nicotine causes an increase in blood pressure and heart rate. Smoking also increases the amount of fatty acids, glucose, and hormones in the blood.

Carbon monoxide from smoking damages the inner walls of the arteries which encourages the buildup of fat on these walls. Smoking decreases platelet survival, decreases clotting time, and increases thickness in the blood. All of these things can lead to a heart attack.

Research shows that secondhand smoke (the smoke from other people's cigarettes) harms the health of people who do not smoke. When nonsmokers breathe cigarette smoke, it can pose serious health risks for them, too. (For example, it can cause breathing problems in children and cancer and heart disease in adults.)

In the United States, more than five million young people now younger than age 18 will eventually die prematurely from smoking-related diseases.

In 1994, research revealed that 30% of three-year-old and 91% of six-year-old children could identify "Joe Camel" as a symbol of smoking.

When people smoke, their skin wrinkles faster, their teeth become stained, they have bad breath, their lungs receive less oxygen, and their taste buds are deadened.

Smoking can also change the effects of medication on the body.

Final Assessment *(cont.)*

Research Guide

Directions: After reading the "Smoking Fact Sheet" on page 136, make three generalizations about the harmful effects of smoking. Then, go to the library and do more research in order to find more support for your generalizations.

Generalization #1:	Sources
1. 2. 3.	
Generalization #2:	**Sources**
1. 2. 3.	
Generalization #3:	**Sources**
1. 2. 3.	

Final Assessment *(cont.)*

Persuasive Writing Graphic Organizer

Directions: Use the following graphic organizer to plan your writing.

Opinion Statement on the Issue:

Key Point #1:

Key Point #2:

Key Point #3:

Concluding Ideas:

Final Assessment *(cont.)*

Prewriting Guidelines

Directions: Use the following checklist to make sure that you are including all of the criteria necessary to write an excellent letter to the editor.

Development and Organization

- ❏ Write a clear opinion statement.

- ❏ Include two or three supporting details for your opinion.

- ❏ Organize your key points in a logical order.

- ❏ Write a clear conclusion that summarizes your key points and extends your ideas in some way.

Style

- ❏ Write a good lead that "grabs" your reader's attention.

- ❏ Vary your sentence length.

- ❏ Use transitions to link your paragraphs.

- ❏ Use specific words and descriptive details so that your reader fully understands what you mean.

- ❏ Use calm, unemotional words and sentences.

- ❏ Use figurative language, if appropriate.

Final Assessment *(cont.)*

Self-Revision Activity for the Final Assessment

Part I

Directions: Reread your letter to the editor carefully. As you read, complete the following exercises.

- ❑ Underline your opinion statement.
- ❑ Circle your support statements.
- ❑ Underline twice your examples from text and personal experience.
- ❑ Put a zigzag line under transitions.
- ❑ Revise any part of your letter that is weakly developed.

Part II

Directions: Respond to the following questions in order to double-check that you have included all the necessary parts of a letter to the editor.

What is my opinion statement in my letter to the editor about the negative effects of smoking?

_____

_____

_____

_____

_____

What are the key points I have included to support my opinion statement?

_____

_____

_____

_____

_____

Did I include important information to support my opinion and key points? Explain.

_____

_____

_____

_____

_____

Final Assessment *(cont.)*

Peer Response Activity for the Final Assessment

Directions: Do the following.

- ❏ Ask your partner to listen carefully as you read your rough draft aloud.
- ❏ Ask your partner to help you improve your writing by responding in detail to the questions below.
- ❏ In the space provided, jot down notes about what your partner says.
- ❏ Make changes, additions, and deletions on your rough draft.

1. What is my opinion statement concerning smoking? _____

_____

_____

_____

_____

2. Have I supported my opinion statement with examples? Give at least one example. _____

_____

_____

_____

_____

3. Did I use good transitions? Give two examples. _____

_____

_____

_____

_____

4. Did I use clear words to express my opinion and state my key points? Give two examples. _____

_____

_____

_____

_____

Final Assessment *(cont.)*

Proofreading Questions

Directions: Use the following questions to guide you in proofreading and editing your final letter to the editor.

Have I used the rules of mechanics so that my audience will take my ideas seriously?

Have I . . .

❑ used proper capitalization?

❑ used correct spelling?

❑ used correct end marks?

❑ used commas correctly?

❑ avoided run-on sentences?

❑ avoided sentence fragments?

❑ punctuated titles correctly?

Final Assessment *(cont.)*

Final Prompt

Directions: Now you are going to write the final draft of your letter to the editor informing children and adults about the negative effects of smoking. Use your rough draft with revisions to guide you.
Remember the following criteria: development, organization, appeals to the audience, style, mechanics, and proper use of technology. Before you begin writing, reread your rough draft one more time for punctuation, grammar, and spelling. When you write your final draft, use additional sheets of paper, if necessary.

_____

_____

_____

_____

_____

_____

_____

_____

_____

_____

_____

_____

_____

_____

_____

_____

_____

_____

_____

_____

_____

_____

Final Assessment Rubric

Directions: Use the following rubric to evaluate the final assessment.

	Self	Peer	Teacher
Development and Organization			
Strong lead that grabs the reader's attention (3)			
Opinion clearly stated (1)			
Adequate support for the opinion statement (2)			
Support arranged in order of importance (2)			
Strong conclusion that ties together key points (3)			
Audience			
Content appeals to audience's knowledge (2)			
Style			
Transitions between paragraphs (3)			
A variety of sentence lengths (3)			
Stylistic elements (2)			
Mechanics			
Correct capitalization (3)			
Correct use of end marks (3)			
Minimal spelling errors (3)			
Minimal grammatical errors (3)			
Correct paragraphing (3)			
Technology Use			
Technology used effectively to draft, revise, and edit (4)			
Total out of 40 points			